THE LINK IN THE CHAIN

The History of a Dutch Jewish Family, Before, During and After WWII

THE LINK IN THE CHAIN

The History of a Dutch Jewish Family, Before, During and After WWII

Judic Wynberg-de Vries

CHERRY ORCHARD BOOKS
2024

Library of Congress Control Number: 2024947671

Copyright © Leo Wynberg, Jack Wynberg, Alice Nagus, and Claire Freeman, 2024

ISBN 9798887196275 hardback
ISBN 9798887196282 paperback
ISBN 9798887196299 ebook PDF
ISBN 9798887196305 epub

Book design by Kryon Publishing Services
Cover design by Ivan Grave

Published by Cherry Orchard Books, an imprint of
Academic Studies Press
1007 Chestnut St.
Newton, MA 02464
press@academicstudiespress.com
www.academicstudiespress.com

Front cover image: Judic and Bram celebrating their
12½ wedding anniversary, 1952
Background image: Lace from de Vries family fabric store
Back cover image: Hotel Wijnberg dining room

Contents

Preface	ix
Prologue	xiii
1. Amsterdam	1
2. Our Meeting	3
3. The Refugees	9
4. Our Engagement	13
5. Tension	15
6. Breaking Up	17
7. Our Wedding	21
8. Our Lost Honeymoon	25
9. One Day on the Front Line	29
10. Tired Soldiers and Nervous Police	33
11. On the Move	37
12. Max and Bram: Soldiers	41
13. Smuggling Merchandise	45
14. The Nazi in the Store	47
15. Anti-Jew Laws	51
16. Sign of the Times	55
17. Medical Examination	59
18. Uncertainty	63
19. A Second Son	65

20.	Family Code	67
21.	Walking Away from Home	71
22.	Trying to Adjust	75
23.	Betrayal...	79
24.	Hiding Out	87
25.	The Trains	93
26.	Were Our Children Safe?	95
27.	An Unreliable Nephew	99
28.	A Reason for Living	103
29.	Needing a Doctor	105
30.	Betrayed Again	109
31.	Our Baby, the Nurse, and Me	111
32.	The Castle in Wapenveld	115
33.	Bram Standing Invisible	121
34.	Secret Police	123
35.	The Park-keeper	151
36.	A Hiding Place	157
37.	A Dangerous Man	159
38.	Radio Orange	161
39.	Hunger Winter—1944	163
40.	Canadian Soldiers	167
41.	Suddenly Free	169
42.	Coming Home	171
43.	So Many Lost	177
44.	Displaced Persons	179
45.	Painful Words	183

46.	The "Safe-Keepers"	187
47.	Our Shul	191
48.	Showing Our Scars	193
49.	Alida's Surgery	197
50.	JAZ—Jewish Amusement Zwolle	201
51.	Hotel Wijnberg	205
52.	Partir C'est Mourir un Peu	209
53.	The New World	219
54.	Starting to Settle	223
55.	Hurricane Hazel	229
56.	Finding Our Place	233
57.	Nightmares	239
58.	Remembering Our Roots	241
59.	Leo and Sheila, Claire and David	243
60.	Jack and Ida	247
61.	Alice and Alan	251
62.	Tradition	253
63.	Ik heb je lief	257
Epilogue		263

Preface

By Claire Carolina Freeman (nee Wynberg)

My mother, Judic Wynberg-de Vries (also known as Jetje, Jetty, Jet, Judith, Tante, Mum, and Oma), started writing this memoir after the death of my father, Abraham Wynberg (Bram, Abe, Oom, Dad, and Opa), in 1977. Like many survivors of the Holocaust, my parents had never opened up to their children (Leo, Jack, Alice and myself) about life before or during the War. When Dad passed away, Mum felt an urgency to tell her story, as one of the few surviving links to that lost life and family in Holland. It became extremely important to her that her children and grandchildren understood where we came from while she could still tell us.

Mum handwrote many drafts of her memoir, always making improvements, typing up pages on a rented manual typewriter when she thought they were good enough—and she kept all of the versions. She filled many coil-bound notebooks with thoughts to be used, and filled many boxes with handwritten, typed, and photocopied papers, sometimes clipping sheets together, and sometimes not.

After Mum passed away in 1998, we four children inherited, among other things, the various drafts of *The Link in the Chain*. I gathered all the documents, diaries, photocopies, and notes I could find. Two large boxes of those documents sat in my home for the next twenty years, essentially untouched. Then in May 2017, thirty-five members of our extended family went to Holland, by invitation of the mayor and the city of Zwolle, for a special Remembrance Day service. It was a powerful and emotional experience that sparked a renewed interest, across the generations, in our family history, and reminded us how fortunate we were to have Mum's memoir. We agreed it was time to work up the manuscript into a book to be shared.

Mum always believed that her memoir was publishable, so over the years she sought out people that might make that happen. However, nervous that her story would be "stolen," she only ever gave prospective publishers a couple of pages, and she copyrighted multiple versions while still writing. Even what I identified as the final typed version of *The Link in the Chain* was marked up with many handwritten notes, inserts, crossings out, and corrections.

The book you are now reading includes all of those last handwritten edits, but very few other edits. We—the family—and the team at Academic Studies Press chose to maintain the cadence of Mum's voice and her distinctive style as much as possible so that the reader can hear her speaking, just as we do when we read her words. For example, while punctuation and most misspellings were corrected, the text retains some spellings and phrasings that are more Dutch than English, such as when Mum adopted the Dutch convention of combining multiple words into one, as in "Davidsstar" and "weddinggown." The only other edits to Mum's text were as follows: we combined some short sentences, paragraphs, and chapters; replaced a handful of words for clarity; removed some repetition; added missing chapter titles; and provided translations of words and names.

Many family members contributed greatly to the publication of our mother's memoir. It could not have come to this point without their vision, passion, dedication, time, and support. For my brothers Leo and Jack Wynberg, my sister Alice Nagus, and myself, this book is a way of fulfilling our mother's wish to give people now and in the future the gift of meeting the past generation. We will be forever grateful for this introduction to family members we never had the privilege to know.

Perhaps because of their tremendous personal losses, our parents made great efforts to ensure that their children remained close, as we have with our own children. All eight of our parents' grandchildren were born within eight years of one another and were always known simply as "the Cousins." They grew up together, even if they lived far apart. It is our belief and hope that they will continue to extend these links in the chain of our family history and keep them strong, through many generations to come.

—May 2024

The Link in the Chain

by

Judith Wynberg-de Vries

Prologue

Holland was a beautiful country, back in the summer of 1937.
The pastures were green, and the cows looked lasy and content. The depression was on the way out and the cities looked cheerfull, with nice stores, old churchtowers, and carillions that played schoolsongs.

And it was that year the meeting place of the jamboree. All young people, from all over the world, in friendship together, in Vandvoort.

And after the jamboree, came more people of good will.
Thousands and thousands, members of the Oxford Group, came to Utrecht.
They had collosal meetings and told us: Improve the World, and begin with yourself.
And everybody cheerfully agreed.

But in Germany the atmosphere was different. And from there came the stories that have to be told.
This, is our story.
remember...

18 July 1985

Prologue in Judic's hand, from original manuscript.

Prologue

Holland was a beautiful country back in the summer of 1937.

The pastures were green and the cows looked lazy and content. The Depression was on the way out and the cities looked cheerful, with nice stores, old church towers, and carillons that played schoolsongs.

And it was that year the meeting place of the Jamboree. All young people, from all over the world, in friendship together, in Zandvoort.

And after the Jamboree came more people of good will.

Thousands and thousands, members of the Oxford Group, came to Utrecht. They had colossal meetings and told us: "Improve the World, and begin with yourself."

And everybody cheerfully agreed.

But in Germany the atmosphere was different. And from there came the stories that have to be told.

This, is our story.

I remember...

— 18 July 1985

1

Amsterdam

There was once, around 1934, in Amsterdam, a Jewish community.

They were colourful, hardworking people, and were part of the non-Jewish population of Amsterdam, who were also hardworking and colourful. They shared a sense of big city humour that was typical Amsterdam. Nobody acted secretive about their outlook on life, and if they had criticism about something, they sure would tell you.

It was still the time that tram conductors were witty and young people respected their schools and their teachers. And if they wanted any reform at all they knew it was meant to let time and personal effort work at it.

There were at that time also thousands of German young men and women working in Holland. They wanted to make some Dutch guilders and send it back home to Germany.

The men usually worked in hotels and restaurants, and the women in households as maids, cooks, or children's care. They were part of the families they worked for.

Suddenly it changed. All young Germans who were working in Holland, most of them in Amsterdam, were ordered by the German government to return to Germany.

The Dutch were surprised. Those German girls that had been part of their family, sometimes for years, became strangers. Had they been spies? What was the meaning of this? And that German, Hitler, what did he want anyway? It was a suspicious fact that all the Germans in Holland obeyed Hitler's order without any comment.

Suddenly they were all packed and gone. Thousands of them. Without an explanation. Without a comment. It was strange.

It must have been coincidence, just part of the course at high school, but during the German language lesson, the teacher wanted us to learn the German national anthem *Deutschland, Deutschland über alles* (Germany, Germany above all).

Young as we were, and not quite sure yet about what was going on in Germany, and in spite of our fear to have trouble with the teacher, we refused. The few Jewish teenagers in the classroom did not want to sing. We behaved correct and quiet, but we refused to sing "Deutschland über alles."

After school we went home, worried what our parents might say, because we were brought up to obey teachers.

To our surprise our parents were approving our decision.

Yes, the sudden and quiet leaving of all those young Germans had made a change. It had been strange. Probably it meant nothing. Probably they needed them to work in Germany. We should ignore it.

It was ridiculous to think that all those waiters and maids could have been spies. They were just workers.

Most of them, anyway. But some of them?

2

Our Meeting

How did we meet?

It was a nice day in the summer of 1937 when the mailman delivered a letter to our home. It came from an old aunt from Zwolle, who invited us to her seventy-fifth birthday party. Dinner with dancing was to be held in Hotel Wijnberg in Zwolle. Pa, Mom Max, my brother, and me, we were all invited.

Pa refused right away. Pa was a well-built man, slightly overweight, with a good head of hair, and a smile that showed a sense of humour. He did not like old aunts, probably, and did not want to leave the store. And Max, who had a store in Zeist, had the same excuse.

So Mom turned to me and asked if I liked to go with her. No, I did not. I was sixteen, shy, and did not like going to old ladies' birthday parties. Probably not one young person there.

But Mom said I could wear again my gold satin evening gown that I had from being a bridesmaid for my cousin Chelly Visser, and the matching gold leather sandals.

Well, Mom and I were going.

Arriving in Zwolle, we went to the house of the old aunt and her two very old sisters. There we dressed up.

Mom looked elegant in a black evening gown, her old golden earrings, and some other good jewellery.

She had wavy silvergrey hair, a young complexion, and a rather slim figure.

Finally, we went by taxi to Hotel Wijnberg.

Coming into the ballroom there I met two cousins from Amsterdam, who were dressed in rich big-city fashion.

And I felt small and finished.

There was only one young man visible, distinguishedly dressed in a black dress suit and white tie. He seemed to belong there somehow.

After a while we were requested to take our places at the dinner table. Then I noticed the young man going around with the hors d'oeuvre plate, from guest to guest.

Suddenly I hear somebody ask me: *"Q'est ce que voulez vous, mademoiselle? Du saumon?"*

And I heard myself answer: *"Un petit peu, s'il vous plaît."*

I looked up, and there was the young man with the black suit and the white tie, who spoke French to me. He had a beautiful smile and his teeth were white and even. His hair was red and wavy.

He went on to the other guests, and when he was ready, he stood across the table from me. We looked at each other, so quiet and good. We seemed to find our home in each other's eyes.

Then the band started to play and there was dancing. And later, there was an announcement about a dancer who would demonstrate a tap dance.

And there he was again, the young man with the red wavy hair, who was the performer. He was good.

Now I went downstairs to powder up, and the bandleader, Chris Bakkers, came there and started some small talk with me. But not for long. There was the young man, and somehow, he seemed to be the only one there.

He asked me if I wanted to go for a walk around the cattle market. I answered I have to ask my mother.

The answer was yes. We walked outside in the summer evening, under a nice moon. I was hoping that a star would shoot and that I could wish to stay some longer, and that he would like me.

In the moonlight he talked softly to me and told me that he talked French to me on an impulse, and that he expected me to understand it. He was just back from working in Brussels, which was French-speaking.

He stroked my arm, and I hoped he would not think me too skinny, or that the soft light hair on my arm was noticeable. His white and even teeth looked beautiful in the moonlight.

When we were almost back at the hotel, there was my mother's worried voice. "Jet, should you not come inside? It is rather cool here." I said, "Yes, Mom." And that was the end of a dreamy beginning.

My mother told me later that she became worried when she realised that she had allowed me to go for a walk with a strange young man. She had gone to Uncle David, who assured her that the young man was quite respectable and the son of the hotel owners. His name was Bram Wijnberg.

The evening came to an end and it had started to rain.

The young man came near the door and looked from the rainy outside to me in my golden evening gown and gold leather sandals.

And then he said: "You cannot go out like that in this weather. I will bring you the coat of my sister, Selma, and you can send it back when you are home again." It sounded so thoughtful and generous that I accepted.

So Mom and I went to the station and took the train back to Utrecht. We sent the coat back with a thank you note.

It did not take long before I got a letter back, starting with "Dear Miss" and finishing with "Respectfully yours." That gave me the chance to write him also, starting with "Dear Sir" and finishing with "Yours truly."

Then he wrote again that he had to be in Utrecht on August 31st and if I would like to spend the afternoon with him.

"Dear Sir, yes!"

And then came August 31, which was Queen Wilhelmina's birthday. It was two o'clock in the afternoon when he stepped in the store, received and looked over by Pa. I went to the store and took him with me to the living room behind the store, where Mom was waiting with coffee and pastry.

Finally, we left home and we tried to talk. He asked: "Where would you like to go?" Because I did not know, and was afraid to show my inexperience, I said no to everything he suggested. But finally we decided to go to Zeist.

It was a fifteen-minute tramride out of Utrecht, and you came to a forest. It was nice there. High pine trees through which the sun filtered down to the ground, onto a carpet of needles.

After we had walked for a while, the sky suddenly darkened and a thunderstorm with heavy rain came down on us. We started to run for the Hunter's Lodge, a restaurant in the middle of the forest.

While waiting for our tea, Bram shook the rain off of his jacket, pulled a comb through his hair, and looked perfect again.

I was intrigued by Bram's easy return to a civilized appearance.

My hairdo had gone limp, my summerdress went limp, and I felt limp.

Gradually we started to go back to the tramstop. Of course, we just missed the one we needed, to be home at six o'clock, as was arranged.

"Knowing Pa's punctuality," I told Bram, "I don't think I go out with you tonight." Bram felt bad, because he thought I did not want to.

But out of the tram, on the way home, Max came to meet us. Max was ten and a half years older than I, and he had come to warn us. He told me: "Jet, you are in for big trouble with Pa. You are ten minutes late and Mom waits with dinner."

Yes, there was trouble. Pa came in the store right at us and shouted at Bram: "Who are you, what do you think taking out a young girl of only sixteen years!" I had just told Bram that I was seventeen, and I cried from shame.

Bram answered: "You could have taken information about me." Then he walked out. In a strange city, not knowing what to do.

Then Mom and Max calmed Pa, and I was allowed to bring him in again. Finally, we were having dinner. Max was terrific. Max was a slim man, with a soft look in his blue eyes, and an easy smile. He tried to help and made conversation, and asked what we were going to do that night. Being the queen's birthday and a holiday.

Max suggested a nice restaurant near a canal, and where there was outdoor dancing on summernights. Tonight there would also be fireworks.

Pa agreed, but only if Max was going with us as a chaperone. So that was decided.

It was a nice evening after a warm day, and the dancing was under a dark-blue sky. The band played softly the new melodies of that time.

It became very quiet just before the fireworks started. Conversation had stopped.

And then suddenly, when a sparkling arrow went in the air, Bram shouted loud: "Ooooh!" And with the next firerainbow, Bram again shouted loud: "Aaaaah!"

And that broke the ice.

He was a hit with Max. When we came home, Mom gave us all coffee and raisinbread, and Bram could stay overnight on the divan downstairs.

Next morning, Bram left.

Bram wrote a little letter to thank us for the hospitality. And so, the correspondence started again.

It was much later, about December, that he came again. This time when Pa suggested that Max should chaperone us, Max answered, "No, Pa, now it is your turn." So, Max finished the chaperone role. When Bram left Utrecht that time, I brought him to the train, and was kissed by him.

It was the first time in my life.

Later on, Max and a girl, and we, sometimes double dated.

3

The Refugees

Utrecht is a fairly big city in the middle of Holland. It has a university, a few canals, and in the centre of the city is a very high Gothic-style churchtower, the Dom. Every year there was a commercial conference in Utrecht, at de Jaarbeurs which drew business people from all over Europe. My parents always went there and sometimes did some business. Buying the newer fabrics that had come out.

In downtown Utrecht, not far from the Dom, we had a large store, well stocked with fabrics and some related articles. Behind the store we had a livingroom and a kitchen, and behind that, there was a long hall leading to a warehouse with three floors.

Above the store we had a huge apartment. Under the stairs was a small office with a big built-in safe. Completely out of sight. Being a real oldtime canal house, it had all kinds of unexpected space everywhere.

Business was good, and besides other help, we all worked in it. Pa, Mom, and I. Max, my older brother, had his own store in the nearby town Zeist.

Although we worked hard, life was good to us.

Everything seemed alright, until you read the newspapers. There were things happening around us, outside of Holland, but very close to it, in Germany.

The Germans persecuted the Jews. And many of the German Jews crossed the border to get refuge in Holland. Utrecht, being in the centre of Holland, might have been getting the most.

Trainload after trainload with refugees came into Holland. They needed homes and food and clothes, and money sometimes.

These refugees came alone, or with their families, and owned just what they could carry. They did not know where to go and what to do after they came off the train. It became a problem.

Then some prominent Jews and business people from Utrecht came together and formed a committee. My father was one of them and lawyer Sanders, who was alderman of Utrecht. They decided to help. The first thing they did was asking for volunteers to be at the station, looking out for possible refugees. My brother Max volunteered. They helped them with their luggage, and supplied food and places to sleep for the first few days. After that, the committee tried to place them more permanently. Or they might travel on to Amsterdam or other cities.

My father, who owned houses, offered one family of refugees—man, wife, and a few growing children—the use of one of his houses for a full year, rentfree. Other Dutch Jews opened their homes and offered their guestrooms and supplied meals.

It was a stream of German refugees who kept coming in, night and day. Some of them, who had come with their families, were sad and worried. They had no prospects and no hope to achieve anything but staying alive. Some tried to obtain jobs or offered their services. There was a young musician who offered music lessons for a small fee or in exchange for clothes and food. He started me on playing the guitar. I had some lessons from him and he always stayed for dinner, and Pa paid him. Some other refugees just tried to keep up their spirits by trying to use their sense of humour. I remember Pa talking to one of those men, who was kibbitzing and telling jokes. Pa asked the man how he could be joking after having left his home and business behind in Germany and had no prospects for the future. The man answered him: "This is the only way to go on. If life is so difficult, and you know nothing anymore, then the only answer is to joke and smile at it, and go on living."

"You will learn," he said, "because antisemitism and Nazism will not stop in Germany only."

But the Dutch Jews did not want to believe that. This was Holland, and that was different, we said.

However, we were reading what was happening in Germany.

Beaten-up Jews, old men, young men, women and children. Ruined synagogues, Jewish homes and stores.

The Germans denied those stories.

"*Es ist nicht wahr*" ("It is not true") became a slogan. Horror tales, they claimed. Propaganda!

There existed in Holland a political party, the National Socialist Movement (NSB) that had similar programs as the Nazi Party in Germany.

When in Holland the next election day came, there were in Utrecht loudspeakers placed all over the city, which broadcasted the results. Everybody came out to listen and was involved with it. The result was that the NSB came out with only 4%. And whenever the NSB was mentioned, there was booing for those 4% only.

Everybody felt relaxed, because it was really a small minority. The Dutch were pleased and went on doing their regular things, and feeling smug that Holland was uninvolved with what was going on in Germany.

Nobody could guess the future.

4

Our Engagement

Bram lived in Zwolle in his family's hotel. On Thursday nights he worked late with the hotel guests who were there for the early Friday morning cattle market. The farmers were early to the market and came in the restaurant at five o'clock in the morning for their first cup of coffee or glass of *genever* to warm up. Bram did not get much sleep. After the market, on Friday night, he came to Utrecht, and stayed with us the Saturday.

Saturday being a big day in the store, I had not much time. It did not occur to us to withdraw from working in our parents' business and just take time off. But my parents were very easygoing. When on Saturday I worked in the store, Bram was in the room behind the store where he fell asleep on the divan. It became a standard joke that when somebody wanted to know what Bram did for a living and asked me: "What does your fiancé do?"

I answered: "He sleeps."

Once on a nice Sunday morning, when Bram had found a nice spot in a park, he said he would like to be engaged with me. I liked that too. And then, right away, I said, "I want a ring."

We went home to tell my parents and Max. Or maybe Bram went first to Pa to ask for my hand.

Sundays the stores were closed. All day long I was useless for any kind of conversation. All I said was, "I want a ring, I want a ring."

Monday morning, we were the first customers at a jeweller, and after choosing two heavy gold bands, we ran out and exchanged rings.

That was 2 February 1938.

Now it was Pa who wanted something. He wanted to make an engagement party for us to make it correct. It was sort of an announcement to family, friends, and business relations that his daughter was not dating. She was respectably engaged to be married.

Invitations were sent out. It became a big affair in the first-class hotel, the Castle of Antwerpen.

We were flooded with baskets of flowers from business people and nice gifts from family and friends. It was an affair that lasted from lunch, then reception, and finally dinner and dancing.

After our engagement party we were involved in choosing breakfast dishes. Ordering matching teacups. Looking at furniture. Our teacups were ordered and had to come from an Eastern European country. It was understood that we had to wait for a long time.

Our business was booming. People bought more than ever before.

Then Germany invaded some countries. When after a while I received my teaset from the same factory as I had my breakfast set from, it did not mention the original country anymore, but was marked: "Made in Germany"!

The Germans had invaded the country and had confiscated the factory. That gave us a beginning of a feeling of tension.

5

Tension

It must have been about that time that Max suggested that we should sell everything and go to America. Our family considered it and made the tragic mistake of deciding to stay. Part of deciding not to leave was that Bram and I were going to marry.

Then Max wanted to go to Palestine. Max did not think it right to stay for the sake of the business, or any other reason. He said that in a dangerous situation absence of body is better than presence of mind.

But Palestine was in our minds a desert, and Max became discouraged and remained in Holland.

There was never another chance. Hitler invaded more countries and Holland mobilized their army. Max and Bram, both soldiers, had to put on their uniforms again. Later on, also Bram's brother, Marthijn.

Lawyer Sanders seemed to have left, and Pa later had a Jewish lady lawyer.

Now, Pa and Max still might have inquired about going to America, but were completely discouraged by their cruel quota system, which was ruthlessly enforced.

Then there were more Jews who felt the need to leave Holland. America had their quota and Switzerland was guarding their borders against refugees.

But the Jews were worried and felt the need to try to leave Holland. The first thing they needed to do was making their assets liquid, changing it into money, gold, or jewellery. Or diamonds. And for that, they had to sell their businesses, their houses, and other properties.

Because many Jews tried to sell, and felt rushed for time, they were not in a good bargaining position. The non-Jewish Dutch buyers knew that.

Thus, some panic selling happened, and good houses, land, or businesses changed hands at squeezed-out low prices.

Pa tried not to sell to *profiteurs*.

The only thing he sold was our huge antique wardrobe that he had bought years before. It was from solid dark oakwood, and a true museum piece. Only in a museum I might have seen a similar one, but never as solid or original as ours was.

And there is a slight memory of a feeling then, that Pa did not really want to sell it, but somehow was persuaded to it.

6

Breaking Up

Bram and I were engaged for about two years. But we did not see each other very often. Bram was in Zwolle and I was in Utrecht. Or for a while I worked in Rotterdam in a Jewish hospital as assistant head of the household. I wanted to learn about household things on a bigger scale, like in a hospital, so that knowledge could be used in running a hotel. For instance, tablesettings, food, and even to *bensj* (*bentsch*, lead the grace after meals) on a Friday night if nobody else was around who wanted to do it. I had been asked to follow the course for nursing and become an RN. But I refused because that was not the reason I worked there.

Bram being in Zwolle and me being in Rotterdam kept us too much separated. I was about half a year in that hospital and did not see Bram very often.

Once, on my day off, I went to Utrecht and Bram came there too. And he broke our engagement.

I did not understand why, and cried. Maybe he felt tied down. He worked very hard for his parents in the hotel. Maybe that made him hesitate to have other obligations. The business of his family depended for a good deal on Bram.

After we broke up, there was no reason for me to stay in the hospital, so I quit.

I went home to Utrecht and worked in the store again.

Although we came from Amsterdam, and I was born there, Pa could not very well breathe the air that came from all the canals there. He had asthma. The family doctor, Dr. Keesing, advised Pa to look for another city to live in. In the meantime, he had to go every year to Bad Ems, a spa in Germany, surrounded by forest. There he felt better. After some years of moving around, Pa noticed that he felt alright in Utrecht. Thus, we settled there.

But now, after eighteen years living in Utrecht, Mom wanted to go back to live in Amsterdam, to be with their brothers and sisters. They rented an apartment in Amsterdam and Pa commuted to the store in Utrecht.

In Amsterdam, I started to work as a correspondent secretary in Dutch and English. I worked for a German blouse manufacturer, who dictated in German! He could not speak Dutch very well, and English not at all. His dictations were impossible to use for business letters. I suggested that he would give me the incoming mail and I would answer it. He just had to sign.

After he started to trust my work, he was quite pleased about that. So was I.

I was pleasantly settled in that office when I got a letter from Bram. He wanted to meet me at two o'clock in Amsterdam in a restaurant. At two o'clock I was still at home. I made sure I looked elegant, and I did not feel like rushing to my ex-fiancé. Mom did not like that I was so slow and too late for my date with Bram. She loved Bram. We all did!

Finally, I left and after another half hour of streetcar riding, I stepped in the restaurant where Bram was waiting for me. He did not mention me being so late. After a hello how are you, Bram ordered coffee and pastry. Then we started to talk. He suddenly said he wanted to get married with me as soon as possible. I might have been a little reserved.

But then Bram told me that he had gone out with other girls and called them all Jetje, no matter what their name was. The girls did not like that, but Bram did not care because it made him realize that we should be together. Bram had looked into a wedding date and wanted it before a Jewish holiday in which you could not make a party. I said yes, but was quiet and thoughtful. We both were.

Then we went to my home, where Bram had to tell my parents. Pa was not quiet, but he was thoughtful. He asked Bram how he had the idea that he could act like he did. Not engaged anymore and then marry so fast. Pa did not care to hurry.

But Bram was determined, and the date before the holidays that would postpone it some more weeks had to be 8 May 1940.

So much had to be done.

7

Our Wedding

Pa took me to his wholesale suppliers and told me I could choose what I liked, and he told the wholesalers to give me the best and send him the invoice.

Then I went on a spree of taking beautiful sheets, pillowcases, tablecloths, and towels. I drove them up the wall because I wanted everything monogrammed in white: A. W. They protested that they never did that, but somehow it was done.

Mom took me to a chic store for a darkbrown woolen tailored skirtsuit with a beige silken blouse for registering for marriage, which had to be done fourteen days before the wedding. Then Mom took me to one of her nieces, who was a high-class milliner. She made for me a darkbrown velour hat with high off of the face brim and a fringed, wide, darkbrown ribbon hanging down on one side. Finishing it off were a pair of brown fashionable heeled leather shoes and soft leather brown gloves. From Bram I had a matching beige leather purse he had given me for my birthday.

Altogether quite elegant.

Mom spent on me in that time before our registering for marriage some golden ten-guilder coins that she had saved for years. The two weeks between registering and the wedding day were called the "bride's days."

Then, for the wedding day, we chose pure white satin and brought that to our dressmaker. For the veil we went again to my mother's niece, who would embroider it around the seams. But because it is a *mitswe* (*mitzvah*, honour) to embroider a bride's veil, there were five or six women working on it and each doing some centimeters. Me, being the bride, it was a must to embroider my share, while we were having tea and cookies later.

Then it was May 7, the day before the wedding. And we got a shock. All passes for soldiers were stopped. That affected Bram, Max, and Bram's brother, Marthijn. There were rumours of German troops nearing the Dutch border, and all soldiers had to be at their station. Bram and Max and Marthijn were as good as prisoners at their stations. Leaving it would mean desertion.

In our home suddenly everything seemed hushed. We were not sure anymore there would be a wedding the next day.

Early in the afternoon Bram's parents came from Zwolle and we asked them and they asked us for more news. Nobody knew what was going on.

Then there came Bram from Amersfoort. He had somehow passed the guards and left.

Right after that, Max came from Soesterberg, where he was stationed. He simply had told them: "I am going to my only sister's wedding. I'll face the consequences when I am back." Then he walked out.

Max later told us that when he came back after the wedding he treated all soldiers to coffee and cookies. They congratulated him and then brought him with jokes, good wishes, and singing to the *petoet* (soldiers' detention).

When the war started he was right away freed to take his place in his army detail. Which was Morse code and radio communication.

Marthijn could not come. He had been ordered to blow up some bridges.

But with Bram with us, we went on with the necessary activities. In the evening, I went to the Great Synagogue near our house. I had to go to the *mikwe* (ritual bath), and was accompanied by my mother and Bram's mother.

After the mikwe, when we came out of the shul, there were some aunts waiting outside and congratulating and going upstairs with us for coffee. It was a real women's evening. My hair that had been done that afternoon was a wet mess.

Bram was not allowed to see me that evening, and was in a hotel. There he had company from some cousins.

But the next morning, against the rule, there was Bram down in the street whistling for me.

I waved and he had to go then. The hairdresser was late and we discovered I needed something old and something blue. Everybody rushed.

And then I was ready.

My head was covered with the veil, and my gown had the train draped around me.

Then the *Gosen* (*chosson*, groom) was allowed in, to meet his *Kalle* (bride).

There he was in his wedding suit, with black silk top hat and gloves in his hand.

His face was white like paper. My God, I still can see his face, so full of love and good promise.

We did not eat anything. We had to fast till after the *goupah* (*chuppah*, wedding canopy).

First we had to go to the registrar's office for our civic wedding. We were half an hour late.

After the civic ceremony, when we were going to the car, Bram sighed and said: "Half safe." He might have been worried about military police breaking it up and taking him back to his military station in Amersfoort.

Then we went with the cars to Hotel Hiegentlich in the Hoogstraat.

Here a rabbi performed the ceremony.

When the glass was broken and everybody called, "Mazel tov," Pa fainted.

Why? Was it his heart, or a worried premonition? I don't know. But at our wedding it was the last time that our families were together.

We had lunch, a reception with a band, and then we went to my parents' home. We said goodbye and I took my little bedroom carpet to take with me to my future home.

This was 8 May 1940.

8

Our Lost Honeymoon

Bram had rented a car, and now we went on our honeymoon to our own home in Amersfoort. Amersfoort was the place where Bram's garrison was stationed.

We were quiet. The bright day had changed into a dark-blue evening with only a few glittering stars. Bram drove steady through this velvet night to our home and future together.

Then we were there. We went into our own home and looked around us. We had an old Finnish-style diningroom set and a brown carpet on the floor and a buffet with a set of imported tea and breakfast dishes. And a beautiful dinner set, a bedroom, and a kitchen given by my parents. A big lounging chair from Max and cutlery from Bram's parents. So much, all new, and beautiful—all ours.

And we had each other. Finally, we were home!

Our home. The home we were starting to live in together. We were going to be together forever, surrounded by loving people and beautiful things.

Quietly we undressed and went to bed. Just to know that we would be together so peaceful for the rest of our lives.

The world could wait.

Could it? Bram tensed up suddenly and said: "I hear somebody knocking on the door. I am going to have a look."

He came back upset. He told me there were some soldiers who wanted him to come back to his army quarters before they missed him. They had covered up for him so far, but could no longer. There were more rumours about the border movements from German troops, and the commandant of Bram's army camp was on the alert that the soldiers were at their posts.

Bram refused to go with them. He told them: "This is my weddingnight and I stay with my wife." The soldiers had to go, but were still warning him.

The next morning, we had breakfast, and then Bram left.

After a few hours he was back again and we had some hot chocolate. And again, he had to leave.

Later he came back for the night.

We were sleeping, in each other's arms, when Bram suddenly was wide awake. "I hear something," he said. "I hear airplanes."

He ran to the windows and opened the curtains. We saw the sky filling up with airplanes. Bram looked, not believing it.

"My God," he said. "Those are German planes. Now I really have to go. This means war!"

Bram kissed me and left. I was not worried: it was so unreal.

But Bram knew it was serious. He was a soldier, and aware of the danger of those German planes flying over the Dutch defense lines.

I don't remember whether he came back that day. I don't really know.

Sometime later, a boy from the Jewish bakery came to tell me that I should leave the house and go with him to the bakery and from there to Utrecht. Because we had no phone, my parents had contacted them.

Germany had declared war on Holland! And Amersfoort was in the firing line.

Bram would get a message where I was. But I had to leave right away. The whole city of Amersfoort had to evacuate. Which means you leave everything behind, and just run away to some place where the danger is not so acute.

I had to leave behind already Bram, my husband. After having been with him only one and a half day! Leaving behind our home, so beautiful a place waiting for two loving people to live in it.

I was dazed and did the first thing that was told to me. I went to Utrecht.

My parents had put up two beds in the store, where they thought was least dangerous for bombing or shooting.

I was afraid. Bram was somewhere else, and here I was in the store trying to sleep.

So scared…

This was 10 May 1940.

Bram and I had had a restless honeymoon of one and a half days.

9

One Day on the Front Line

———

Sunday. Was it May 12? Pa said: "We are going to look for Bram and maybe Max. Bram in Amersfoort, Max in Soesterberg. We are going on our bicycles." So we started to ride. It was strange. Everybody had left, or was leaving from the direction that we were going. Some people warned us. "Go back! Don't go to Amersfoort! You will meet Germans." Or they said: "Amersfoort is empty! You can go nowhere! The roads are blocked!" So many rumours. You did not know what to think.

Pa said: "We are going on, we are going to see for ourselves." I do not remember how long it took us. We did not see Max in Soesterberg. But we came in Amersfoort, and we came to our home.

When we got in, we found a note from Bram, that he knew where I was. Bram, all through our lives, always knew where to find me.

Pa suggested that I should have an opportunity to see Bram. He inquired and found out where Bram was stationed.

Pa and Mom brought me there, and then stayed behind to wait for me.

Bram was in the front line!

I walked down there, and the soldiers let me walk there, knowing I was Bram's wife of three days and that Bram was in the front line. But at a certain spot I was not allowed any further. The guards sent a message to Bram, and I had to wait.

Bram came to me. My God, Bram was there. And it was war. I could not absorb it. It was all wrong.

We did not have long. Bram had to return to his bunker. He knew I could not stay in Amersfoort because it was evacuated.

We both were deeply impressed that we could not stay together and were separated so soon again. And that there was war and danger.

But we kissed and had to say goodbye again.

After I had said goodbye to Bram, I went back to Pa and Mom and we got on our bicycles to go back to Utrecht. (We did not see Max.)

I had to leave Bram behind, there, in the front line.

Years later Bram told me how dangerous it had been for him.

Our Dutch soldiers were young men that came from their farms, business, or jobs. Although trained when enlisted, they were not military-minded and unfamiliar with war. They were uninformed and not sure what was happening. But they tried their best and were on the alert.

When it became darker, their eyes tried to look through the bushes that were surrounding them. Whenever they saw a move or heard a noise, they started shooting. They did not know that there were two lines of bunkers and the bullets of the second line came in the Dutch trenches ahead of them, endangering their own men. The soldiers in the front trenches, who were looking out for the enemy in front of them, were being shot at by their own men in their backs. That had to be stopped.

The men in the endangered bunker drew straws.

Bram was the one who had to go out in the night, risking the bullets that came from everywhere. He had to reach the bunker behind them and inform them about their position.

And while he was crawling out there, alone in the night, his thoughts were with life and death. He asked God: "Is this all I have? Only one night with my wife? Is this my fate? Will this be the end?"

Bram reached the bunker and explained the situation to the commander. Then he had to crawl back to his own station.

Bram had done what needed to be done. He always did. It was part of his life's philosophy.

10

Tired Soldiers and Nervous Police

The day after we came back from Amersfoort, Pa wanted to see our apartment in Amsterdam.

He rented a car with driver and we started to go from Utrecht to Amsterdam.

That trip could have been the scenario for a movie.

But this was reality! And so sad. After only a few a days of war, our army, the Dutch army, all nice young men, were worn out. They had to walk from Soesterberg to somewhere else, and from Utrecht to somewhere else.

Later on, we heard that the soldiers from Amersfoort had left and walked to Maarssen because the German troops were marching up to Amersfoort. So the Dutch soldiers walked from everywhere.

They walked and had their weapons to carry, mortars to pull, and cannons and food and munition.

They walked, and they walked . . . We saw them on the road. Thousands and thousands of them. They looked so forlorn and tired. Nobody knew exactly where to go, or why. Some officer, or order, put them on the move. Not good here. Not sure about where to go. And so they walked, not really able to march.

There were military roadguards along the road to watch out for German spies or suspicious-looking people. They stopped everybody and questioned them. You had to say the word *Scheveningen* correct to prove you were *Hollander*. The thought was that no German could pronounce that right.

Finally, we came in Amsterdam. There we heard some shooting. And there were more nervous guards. Everybody saw in somebody else a traitor from the NSB (Dutch Nazi Party) or German spy.

We went up to our home at the Jonas Daniel Meyerplein. A well-known square with on one side the Great Synagogue and on the other side the well-known Portuguese Synagogue.

Not far from our home was a canal, the Herengracht.

Mother and I went upstairs to our apartment. After a while we noticed Pa had not come home yet. Mom got worried and went downstairs again to see where Pa was. She was back upstairs right away, looking worried. "Go with me to the police station, Jet. They took Pa there."

Why? What was going on?

Mom and I came to that police station. And there was Pa, white and upset. The police had taken him at gunpoint for questioning.

What had happened was that somebody had seen a middleaged man throw some leather, official-looking briefcase in the canal. It looked suspicious. So some people started to look for that man. My father was just down there on his way to come upstairs.

He was suspected and arrested.

Everybody was nervous and overreacting. It took Pa some explaining and phoning and more explaining, and business relations and friends who could identify him, to assure those police officers that he was a Dutch Jew that lived there. Not a German spy or NSB member.

It had taken only a few days of war to disrupt the typical easygoing Dutchman and change him into a suspicious stranger.

***

We stayed overnight in our apartment in Amsterdam. During the night we heard some more shooting and bombing.

The following morning, we heard the terrible news. Rotterdam had been bombed flat! The radio might have broadcasted it, but the rumour was that Amsterdam would be next.

What to do, where to hide? From bombs, and a population that did not trust each other anymore.

Did another night go by? I don't remember how.

But then it was May 14. It was Bram's birthday, but nobody thought about that.

It might have been afternoon that the radio told the Dutch people that the Dutch army had surrendered. That it would be in our own interest, the Dutch people, to behave correct, because the Germans were now boss in Holland.

Pa again took the initiative. He said: "We have to leave Holland before it is overrun by the Germans. We Jews are not safe now anymore."

And then Max came home. He took off his military uniform and changed into civilian clothes. Later on, he buried his uniform.

A dangerous move. Because then the Germans might call him an underground fighter. Which he became later.

Now Max agreed with Pa to leave.

Putting it in the words: "Absence of body is better than presence of mind."

11

On the Move

So, Pa tried to rent a cab. Not one available and no cabdriver wanted to move anywhere.

Then there was the question: Where could we go? The south and east were taken by the Germans, the north did not seem possible somehow, and all that was left was the west.

The North Sea! Possible to cross that and go to England. Thinking about a harbour, IJmuiden seemed favourable.

Again, trying for a cab, Pa found one that wanted to bring us part of the way.

And so, we started our journey. Without another thought about our homes that we left behind us, our business, and our whole way of living.

Only a few days before we had all filled our place in a regular society. But after just a few days of war, it all seemed to be past and lost.

I wanted Bram to go with us, but it was impossible to search for him in this chaotic country. Time was running out.

Pa promised me Bram would be taken out of the country and united with me right after we set foot on shore in England.

We started to ride. The roads were crowded with fugitives in cars, on bicycles, and walking. It was not only the Jews who were afraid for their lives from the Nazis. There were also political prominent people who were known to be anti-Nazi. There were stage and radio artists and writers who had made themselves a name with their ridicule of Hitler. Everybody was afraid and on the move.

We came gradually out of the centre of the city and came to the IJ. The IJ is an Amsterdam harbour connected with other waterways and which divided Amsterdam.

And there came a shock. Across the water was a fire! The flames were skyhigh and the fire seemed kilometers long. A fire caused by sabotage from Amsterdam citizens who had blown up the oil reservoirs from the BP and Shell.

The reason was that they did not want that the oil should come in the hands of the German army.

There was the road on one side with unending rows of cars, bicycles, and other vehicles. And people walking.

And on the other side a wall of flames, lighting up the sky and reflecting on the road. It made light and dark silhouettes on the moving crowd.

People were moving with their eyes fixed on the road ahead of them. Some were waving for a ride. But everybody tried to escape from this nightmare. We could feel the fear and tension surrounding us.

How long we were on that road I don't know. But we came in IJmuiden. IJmuiden is a little harbour and fishertown.

There, the nightmare had a different colour. It was dark. The houses and stores were all tightly closed.

We went to the shore and heard rumours that there was a boat under steam, ready to leave for England.

In this strange dark we started looking for that boat. It did not take long to find it. There was a middle-size boat filled with people, just sitting and standing there, waiting to go and be saved.

We stepped aboard. The boat was warming up already, with the motors running. But we did not move. The captain was not aboard yet.

The rumour went around that money had to be collected from the people to pay for their trip. But nothing was done yet.

It took a while before we became nervous. In the dark we saw farther away the headlights of cars coming into IJmuiden.

Suddenly everybody panicked. They started to push and shout: "The Germans are coming! The Germans are coming!"

"They will shoot us. We are trapped and an easy target on the boat."

Everybody wanted to get off.

When the cars passed and nothing happened, the same panic started again, but now everybody wanted to go back on the boat again.

The boat was still under steam and the engines were still working as if ready to go. But no captain came aboard.

A few young people did not trust it anymore. "Let us take the lifeboats and row to England if we have to."

They started to lower the lifeboats in the water and filled them up to capacity.

And they started to row.

To row a lifeboat in the rough North Sea!

It did not take long when we already heard that some had capsized in the crossing tides.

How many boats and how many people were lost, I don't know. Much later we heard that only one lifeboat really had made it to England. The rumour was that they had been rescued by a fisherboat.

In the meantime, there were more people of the opinion that sitting there in that boat seemed strange and wrong.

My family decided to go back to shore and see if we could find a hotel or home where we could sleep. No, was the answer, if there was an answer.

The people from IJmuiden remained closed and dark.

It became eery, and Pa, in the morning, tried to get back to Amsterdam.

There were more fugitives of the same feeling, but when they went back to the quay where they had left their cars and other belongings, it was all gone!

Later we heard that that boat had the engines running all night but could have not gone anywhere. The harbour had been blocked with sunken ships...

IJmuiden? Dark. Very strange.

12

Max and Bram: Soldiers

Back in our home in Amsterdam, we started to discuss what to do now. The best thing seemed to be to act as if nothing had happened, and try to be inconspicuous. So Max went back to his army camp in Soesterberg. There, the Dutch soldiers put together another uniform for him, to replace the one he had buried. Now he was one of them again. And Pa went back to the store in Utrecht.

So everything seemed normal again.

Bram sent me somebody to tell me that he was now in Maarssen. The Dutch army had to leave Amersfoort before the German troops had arrived there. No matter how tired they were they had to walk to Maarssen.

After Holland had surrendered, there came right away the German order that all Dutch soldiers had to hand in their weapons.

Being prisoners of war now, hiding a weapon would be treated as treason and be punished by death.

Bram kept his revolver (and gun).

So did Max. But Max also had gathered some other weapons and munitions.

It must have been then already that Max started to think in terms of resistance. Bram might have thought about defending the family or me and himself. Both were a good shot.

After some weeks had gone by, Max took Bram and me deep into a forest and showed us where he had buried a few guns and some revolvers with munition. He wanted us to know where we could find them in case we might ever need them.

Max, a young man, with love and a feeling of responsibility.

Knowing now where Bram was, I took my bicycle every day to go to Maarssen to see him. About eight kilometers to go and eight kilometers back. Sixteen kilometers just to see each other for a short time.

We belonged together. But since our one and a half day of tension-filled honeymoon, we never had lived in our home or had any other place where we could have some rest together and feel peace. Every day after our short meeting we had to separate again.

Because I was already living with my parents again, I could not feel that I was a married woman. For Bram, I was at that time the only connection to a life he belonged to, but from which he was separated.

We accepted it, thinking it was related to the general upheaval. We hoped the future would make it all right again.

Nobody knew how long Bram's garrison had to stay in Maarssen. That now depended on orders from the Germans.

But after the Dutch soldiers had handed in "all" their weapons, they gradually were sent home as civilians again.

My parents and Max moved from the apartment in Amsterdam to a house at the Koningsweg in Utrecht.

Bram and I went back to live in Amersfoort. Bram seemed still to have a few weeks back pay coming to him from being a soldier. It was not much, but we lived on that, carefree. We were together and we were young. Expecting his pay on Monday, on Saturday night, from the last few quarters we had left, I bought some candies and for each of us a little cake to have with our tea or coffee. We had a home and all was right and we were together.

But Pa and Mom were older and wiser. One day Pa talked to me and told me he had some merchandise he could not use in the store. Some small lace collars, etc. Would I mind clearing it out for him and sell it? As payment I could keep the intake.

Of course I did not mind. So our income grew and Pa complimented me how well I did.

After a while Pa suggested that we should come to live in Utrecht in one of his houses, and we all should work together in our big store.

It would be an improvement and Bram said yes.

Looking back through the years, that very short time in Amersfoort, in our dreamhouse, serving cheap candies on an elegant silver dish, our life was good.

But we moved to Utrecht and from then on, we waited for our fate to unfold before us.

13

Smuggling Merchandise

For a while it seemed to go normal. There were, of course, German soldiers everywhere. In the streets, in the stores and restaurants.

On the surface they behaved correct, as was instructed them from higher German commands. But there were already rumours about Dutch people being knocked down by Germans for some slight or imaginary insult, like not letting a German pass first or not stopping for him to let him into an elevator. The shopkeepers were especially harassed. When the Germans did not like the service, they messed up the store and behaved threatening to the shopkeeper. They did pay, however, because looting was not allowed to them. Again, high German orders.

But we had to accept their war money for "the best of everything." And they sent their purchases *heim* to Germany.

The shopkeepers tried to avoid selling to the Germans and were sometimes hiding part of their merchandise. The regular Dutch customers were well treated from merchandise that was stocked in the cellar, out of sight of the Germans.

But it did not take long before the stores started to look bare. And buying from wholesalers or factories became difficult. Our store could not supply for the demand, and the wholesalers were in the same position.

Then a different way of doing business started for us. We found a way.

Max or Bram went to other cities and bought there from big stores at regular retail prices, to keep our stock at a fair level.

What they bought they put in a regular piece of luggage and took it with them on the train.

It worked only for a short time. There were more storekeepers doing that and the Germans made it illegal.

They put *Grüne Polizei* (Green Police) at the stations and everybody with luggage had to open it. It became dangerous.

Once, when Bram arrived at the station in Utrecht, his luggage loaded with purchased fabrics, the traveller right in front of him got stopped by the Green Police. He had to open up his luggage and packages to be checked for smuggling.

Bram was right behind him and the next one to be searched.

It was a dangerous situation.

Bram kept his cool. Instead of trying to slip through, which would have been noticed, and look suspicious, Bram put his luggage down, stood still, and acted curious about what was going on.

One Grüne Polizei who noticed that was irritated and urged him: "Come on, get going!"

And then Bram took his luggage and calmly walked on, passing the Green Police.

Bram, intelligent under stress.

14

The Nazi in the Store

We had a big store in the heart of Utrecht. Yes, there was harassment from the Nazis. When they came into a store, they acted powerful. It happened to me. We being Jewish, I was scared.

One afternoon, while Pa, Mom and I were busy in the store, a big Nazi officer walked in. It was a strange sight to see that Nazi in a fabric store. He was tall and had a slightly sour face. He walked straight up to me. He told me he wanted fabric for a coat for his girlfriend in Berlin. It had to be the best and the most beautiful fabric we had.

I told him that I would show him some fabrics and colours and that he could choose. It was not difficult to do that because Pa always bought the latest and best fabrics. So I started to show him one bolt of fabric after the other. All of the best that was available.

But he did not approve of any of it. I did not try to convince him like I would with our regular Dutch customers, but I looked around for other fabrics we might have in the store somewhere.

And I found somewhere in a corner a few pieces of a woolly fabric in a strange off-beige colour. We did never show it in our store.

But being on the end of my imagination I did show it to the Nazi. Somehow he believed that I finally gave him from a hidden treasure, and he told me he wanted some meters from that fabric, enough for his girlfriend in Berlin to make a coat from it. Then he paid and left.

Two weeks later there the same big Nazi officer walked in the store, but this time he had with him another big Nazi officer like a reinforcement. Also, the parcel with the fabric in it. Both, as officers, were fully armed with revolvers.

They came straight up to me. I was scared. It looked as if they came to take me away.

But I just stood there and approached him in what I hoped looked a natural way.

Then he threw the package he had with him on the counter and told me I had given him not what his girlfriend wanted and she had written him that nobody in Berlin was wearing it.

It came down to it that I had fooled a Nazi officer. He sounded dangerous and his fellow officer was showing his support for his friend.

I was scared. I had shown him the best and he had not believed me, and now he came back in his threatening behaviour. Although I did not know yet about the death camps, I was scared.

But suddenly I despised him and his girlfriend in Berlin. I became angry and reacted accordingly.

I asked him if his girlfriend in Berlin knew anything about the fashions that were coming in from Paris and Vienna and Brussels. Berlin, because of the war, might not have received them yet, but we had.

I pulled the fabric from his parcel, walked to before the counter, unfolded it, threw it over my shoulder, and let the extra fabric fall down to the floor.

Then I took from our counter a piece of darkbrown fabric, made a big belt of it around my waist, and let also the extra fabric fall down to the floor, to accent the colour contrast.

The effect was theatrical and they looked impressed and approving. I had often shown fabrics this way.

Nothing was said or done anymore. I packed his fabric up again and I handed it back to him.

They both left.

After a while, when I finally looked around in the store again, there were my parents, standing in a corner, hand in hand, with pure white faces. As a Jew, you don't argue with a Nazi officer.

Mom stammered something like: "You should not have." Pa said nothing.

I am glad I had handed it back to him. It was maybe the only way out of a threatening situation. If someone has forced your back against the wall, the only possibility might be trying to do a step forward.

My parents, who must have realized the danger more than I did, had not interfered with me. But I still remember Pa and Mom standing together, in the corner of their own store, and so white and so afraid for me.

So afraid for me.

15

Anti-Jew Laws

Finally, it happened. We had expected it right away, and when it did not happen, we thought they would not do it in Holland. Then the order came and the first anti-Jew law.

Jews had to wear a big yellow Star of David with the word "Jew" written on it in mock Hebrew lettering. Not wearing it was punishable. Jews were not allowed outside after eight o'clock. Not even in the backyard. Everybody had to have an identity card, and the Jews had a big black "J" printed on it.

The Dutch people reacted by greeting the wearers of the Jewish star with extra politeness. It was nice of them, but it made us feel so singled out.

Jews were not allowed in parks and theaters, or anywhere that they could mix with Aryans. "Aryans" meant people of pure Germanic or Teutonic blood.

It was about this time that we heard that a Jewish shopkeeper, a German refugee who was married to the daughter of a rich Dutch wholesaler, had committed suicide together with his wife. The young woman, whose parents we knew very well, was six months pregnant.

The Dutch Jews were angry at the German refugee, and blamed him that he probably had talked his young Dutch wife into taking that desperate step, taking also the life of the unborn child.

But when time went by, and we felt more of the crippling German laws against the Jews, we started to wonder if that German Jew had a better insight into what was going to follow. Maybe he wanted to protect them from falling into Nazi hands. Having already escaped from Germany to Holland, he might have known more than the Dutch Jews did at that time.

More anti-Jew laws. The Jews were not allowed to own stores.

That uprooted us.

Aryans who applied for your business at some Nazi office, could come in, and you just had to walk out and leave behind your property and your livelihood of twenty or thirty years.

The stock, and even the money in the till, were confiscated.

When it happened to us, our store was very well stocked. We had to leave it all behind, and had to walk out with nothing.

We had never seen before the man who had applied for our store. He had a store already, but he wanted our business. He was impressed with our stock and the volume of our business, and handed Pa about one hundred guilders, to soothe his own conscience. And that was all.

I cannot even guess the value of our business at that time. The quality and quantity of our merchandise, and the goodwill that had built up in more than twenty years of doing business, had a value that could not be estimated with a single pricetag.

Pa, Max, and Bram had tried to save and hide some merchandise in a hurry. Maybe in order to sell or trade in later for necessities.

Pa also had bought some old gold, like broken watches, gold chains, and rings. Maybe for bribes or to keep us alive later on.

Then, something I had hoped for was going to happen. I was expecting a baby.

But when time went by, and always new anti-Jewish laws came into force, I did not feel safe anymore in our own home, and so we were often at the Koningsweg house with my parents and Max. And I was there when the labourpains started.

Mom phoned our Jewish doctor, Dr. Perel. It was after eight o'clock and as a Jew he was not allowed outside.

Dr. Perel phoned some German headquarters. He told the German officer who answered him: "I am a doctor and a Jew. I have a Jewish patient that needs me. Am I allowed to go there after curfew?"

The answer was no.

Then Dr. Perel told the German officer: "I am first a doctor, and I will do my duty and act as a doctor. If you find it your duty to arrest me, that will be your decision. I go to my patient. Now!"

And Dr. Perel came.

After Dr. Perel knew about the timing of the pains, he ordered right away a taxi. Another offense against a law. Jews were not allowed to use public transportation. But he got one.

The doctor, Bram, and I went to the hospital. My parents followed walking.

It was Saturday afternoon, July 19. Before I left for the hospital, and it being our first baby, I asked my mother if she thought it would be born that day. Mom said: "Yes, it will be a Shabbos child, and if it is a boy, it will have his *brith hamilo* (circumcision) on Shabbos. That will be a *mitswe* (*mitzvah*, religious commandment), because otherwise you cannot use a knife on Shabbos to cut and that makes the child special in a good way.

In the hospital, with Bram at my side, our son was born. I shouted once in pain, and my mother heard it outside somewhere and she said to Pa: "This is the birthcry. We have a grandchild."

And we named him after Bram's father, Shemoijl. And Leonard.

And Leo had red hair!

Right away I asked for my purse, combed my hair, and put on some powder and lipstick. When Dr. Perel just came in. I apologized for being so vain at that moment. He gave me a big smile and told me that it was just perfect for a young mother.

When I was in my room in the hospital, there was everybody. I got my baby in my arms, and later the nurse gave Bram our baby in his arms.

And there was Bram, full of awe, looking down at our baby. The son of himself and me!

Soon after that day, Mom got very busy. She was going to have the brith hamilo in their home. Yes, it was on Shabbos. Invited were the doctor, the *moheil* (*mohel*, the specialist who does the circumcision), Bram's mother, and Marthijn. And there was Max.

Bram's mother was the *gefatterin*. That is the woman who has the honour of bringing the baby from the crib to the mohel.

Pa assisted the mohel.

At a time that everything became scarce, my parents made a luncheon so plentiful and so beautiful that everybody forgot their fear and all the dangers outside.

Inside was *simcha* (joy)!

16

Sign of the Times

For the Jews who lived in fear and uncertainty, there was not much possibility to escape the tension or to relax. Also, the telephone lines were disconnected. No exchange of thoughts or information was possible.

Strange as it may seem that in that time of fear and danger, there was such a strong need for diversion.

But the Jews were not allowed in parks, theaters, movies, or anything that might mean mixing with Aryans. All Jewish entertainers, movie actors, bandleaders, musicians, and stage actors were also prohibited to perform for mixed audiences.

In Amsterdam there were quite a few high-quality entertainers from Germany and Holland. They decided to form a group and perform for strictly Jewish audiences only.

The leader of the orchestra was the very well-known composer and bandleader Willy Rosen from Germany. Then there was Max Ehrlich from UFA, the German movie studio. All the others were also big names in the movie and entertainment world. They had rented a theater and gave live stage shows for Jews only.

They called themselves the Prominents. And the theater was the Theater of the Prominents.

They had no access to money or props or costumes. They performed on a bare and scarcely lit stage. They wore their regular streetclothes, sometimes fancied up with a feather stole or a straw hat. But they were overflowing with talent and wit.

It was probably the best entertainment in Holland at that time.

Their language on stage was mixed German and Dutch. Both languages were all broken up. But they came through, sharp. Their dialogues were up to date. Their songs would have been hits in any other time. They had sketches and music.

The word got around, and even the German soldiers and non-Jewish Dutch tried to sneak in.

Max told us about that theater and the show.

Bram and I wanted to forget for a few hours the dangerous circumstances and confined surroundings that we were living in and make-believe everything was normal. We went to the Theatre of the Prominents. We enjoyed the show and admired the unbelievable spirit and the quality of the performance by the actors and musicians. And the grateful understanding of the audience.

We only went once. We escaped death. Because right after that, at another performance, the Nazis found it an easy trap for a raid. They just surrounded the place and took everybody. The audience and the performers.

It is strange that when you are down, and even in danger, that you need and look for amusement. We did not even realize the risk. We needed to escape the tension and the fear for just a few hours.

From concentrationcamp Westerbork, Max wrote us one letter and he mentioned in that letter the names of the Prominents actors who were there at the same time. They had to perform there to amuse the Nazis.

Maybe that postponed their deaths a short while. Only a short while.

Because they were all Jews.

***

After the brith homilo of Leo, we went back to our own home again. On Monday mornings Pa was supposed to collect our rent. Instead, he enjoyed to come in for a cup of fresh coffee, and always brought something with him. Sometimes fresh bread, sometimes fish or cheese. I wanted to pay him, but when I asked the price, the answer was always the same. A few words in some oldtime language, but it meant: "Hold onto your money."

Leo, being the first-born son, should have a *pietjan haben* (*pidyon haben*). This is a ceremony that refers to the times that there was a temple and young boys were obliged to work there and serve the *Kohens* who were the priests. One could free the boys of that duty by paying the priesthood some money.

Now this is only done symbolically. But Leo being our first-born, we liked to have the ceremony, in which some money changes hands to buy him back from the priestservice.

For the ceremony you could choose a friend who was named Cohen, and he would receive ten silver guilders, which usually went to charity. Or you looked for a poor Kohen who could use the money himself.

There were at that time a lot of German refugees who could use it. And Bram found a German Kohen who used to be rabbi in a synagogue in Hamburg. We were very happy with the thought that it would really be a correct ceremony, and my parents wanted to be there too.

But the rabbi was in a hurry. He rushed it and did not want to wait.

He said some prayers, and wished us that we would live to see our son to bar mitswe, marriage, and good works.

Bram paid him and he left right away. Maybe he was afraid to be out after curfew.

My parents came too late for the ceremony. They had walked all across the city because Jews were not allowed to use public transportation.

They were very disappointed and very tired.

The table that had been set with cake and other things remained untouched.

Although the ceremony had not been very special, I still feel bad that they had missed it.

17

Medical Examination

A few months went by. Food became scarcer and was rationed. Bread, sugar, coffee, tea, and meat, and all the everyday necessities were no longer available if you did not hand in your ration coupon together with your money.

New anti-Jewish laws came in force. Jews were not allowed to have radios. We had two radios, but Pa had to deliver them at some German office. That left us without up-to-date news and information that might be important to us. Jews could not have telephones and would be disconnected.

It became clear what was happening. The Nazis were separating the Jews from the rest of the Dutch population by breaking up all forms of communication. The Jews came to stand apart and alone. It was frightening.

It had an ominous and evil atmosphere about it, and uncertainty and waiting.

We had not been waiting so long, when it came. Big articles in the newspapers and proclamations everywhere.

The Jews will be deported! They would have to go to workcamps and be made useful. It would be the "Final Solution" to the "Jewish problem"!

Nothing bad, they said, just work in camps somewhere in Eastern Europe.

And their families could go with them!

And to make it efficient, all men had to be tested by doctors and screened for usefulness and ability.

All Jewish men had to come to an office, where they had to undress and where German doctors would examine them.

Soon we were to distrust the efficiency of the medical checkup when we heard that Jews with severe disabilities were found suitable for the camps. It was a bitter joke that they had just approved a Jew with a wooden head!

Every Jew reacted to his own circumstances and feeling and outlook.

Dr. Perel, an aristocratic man, refused to undress. He told the German doctors: "I am a doctor. I am healthy and capable to go to your camps. Just don't touch me!"

Chief Rabbi Tal from Utrecht was a similar proud kind of man. But most of us showed their fear and worry and tried to fake some illness. They drank lots of coffee and complained to the Nazi doctors they had a bad heart. And some more complicated ways to simulate a sickness or disability in order to be rejected for camp and deportation. But it seldom worked.

Bram was also thinking if it was maybe possible to fake something or do something that he might be rejected.

He wrote his cousin, Izak Cohen, the skinspecialist, who had a big practice in Apeldoorn, if he maybe knew about some symptoms that he could fake which would give the impression of disability, so he would be rejected and be able to avoid deportation.

Izak answered him and sent him some prescription for an ointment. He wrote Bram to rub that ointment on the high inside of his thighs. "Rub it hard in with a brush!"

Izak advised Bram to say nothing, but go to a doctor and show it. Then he might get from a doctor a letter to prove him not suitable.

Bram went to an apothecary and obtained the ointment. Then he brushed it in. He did that quite a few times a day. His skin became red and irritated. It must have caused him quite some pain.

But for a few days he went on, taking the ointment and rubbing, brushing and beating it in. The result was terrible!

He got swollen legs and hundreds of little blisters. And out of all those blisters was oozing pus!

It was wet and fatty and blistered and discoloured. It was a nauseating sight!

Then Bram was ready to go to a doctor. To make it more authentic, he went to a reputable dermatologist.

And there he told that specialist that he had a disease, and if the doctor please would have a look and give him a letter which would tell the Germans about it. Then Bram undressed partly, and showed the skin specialist his blisters and the pus and fatty discolouring and sickening appearance of it all!

The specialist looked at it. Then he looked at Bram.

He said to Bram: "This is a fake. I recognize it."

Bram became worried. Was this stranger going to betray him?

The doctor told him, "I know how you caused this. It must have been Izak Cohen who gave you the prescription. Because outside myself, he is the only one who knows.

We were both assisting a professor who did experiments with ointments. The professor, and Izak, and I were the only ones that worked with this one."

Then, out of respect for his colleague and their professor, the dermatologist gave Bram a letter for the German doctors. In it was an explanation from the specialist that Bram seemed to have an uncommon and hard to treat form of a disease. And he was afraid it might be contagious!

The German doctors kept Bram at a safe distance and sent him home as unacceptable!

Of all the doctors in town, Bram had unknowingly chosen the only right one. We accepted it as coincidence.

Thank God, we had gained some time.

After Bram stopped abusing it, his skin healed perfectly.

18

Uncertainty

The time gained was not without fear. The Jews started to understand that what was really happening was that they were in fact deported to an unknown fate somewhere in Eastern Europe. The screening was just to blur their real plans.

Then the board members of the synagogue in Utrecht called a meeting for all the Jews they could contact. Max and Pa went.

After a few hours they came home and almost whispered what the meeting was all about.

The heads of Utrecht's Jewry indicated, without saying it in so many words, that it would be wise to disappear in any way you saw possible.

Those Utrecht Jews who arranged that meeting shared their fears with the members of their Jewish community, and warned them, and discussed possibilities, and deserve our respect. They had shown to be responsible leaders when they themselves with their congregation faced a dangerous but unknown future.

It was the last time that the congregation, as such, was together.

***

The circumstances we were living in were strange to the lifestyle we were used to. Every day we experienced something that made us feel different.

Pa wanted to know an opinion outside of our family. Other Jews who had maybe made plans whether to stay, trying to leave or trying to hide out. Whatever way would be possible to escape. But nobody knew anything for certain. So Pa went to his new Jewish lady lawyer and wanted to know her opinion about the situation and what could be done. She answered him: "Mr. de Vries, whatever we do will be wrong."

A few days later, in the middle of a conversation, the telephone went quiet. Then we found out that all Jews were disconnected.

Again, this was something that made the Jews feel more separated and alone.

19

A Second Son

Then I found out that I was already a few months pregnant again. Because I had been nursing Leo, we had not noticed it before. For the time being we could not do much. So another half year went by. We noticed that some Jewish families did not live in their homes anymore.

Gradually the date of birth came and we had to make arrangements with the hospital.

Bram, my parents, and Max were very quiet during this time, but very sweet.

Finally, I went to the hospital, and this time only Bram went with me. I did notice it, but accepted it without questioning it. Other things were occupying my mind.

Another son was born, and finally my parents and Max came to visit me.

And then I heard what had really been going on in the meantime. Pa had been summoned to appear before a German court. He did not know the reason. But he did not expect ever to come home again. He even had prepared himself by wearing some extra underclothes.

Because the summons was at the same time as the birth of the baby was due, they hid their despair from me and did not tell me about it. They did not want to frighten their wife, daughter, sister in her labourpains!

Some love, some courage.

Now Pa told what had happened to him.

First, they let him wait in a room. Later on, he discovered it had a mirror by which the Nazis could observe the persons, but it was not noticeable in the room where they were waiting.

Then, when Pa had to appear in court, they accused him of having held back one of our two radios. Thank God Pa could prove he had handed in both radios.

And only now it could be told to me.

We named our son Itschak Menachem (Jack), after Pa and Max. He had dark unruly hair and two crowns, which means good luck.

Again we had a brith hamilo. And again Pa assisted the moheil. He boasted that his grandsons were so strong!

When, as tiny infants, I used to put Leo and, later, Jack in their carriage, outside in the fresh air and sun, I used my bridal veil to cover their carriage, according to Mom's tradition, as a protection against flies and mosquitoes.

Max built clandestine a small crystal radio to receive the news about the movements of the war and to keep in touch with the rules the Nazis made against the Jews.

Our family was still together...

20

Family Code

We lived in Utrecht. Jews were not allowed to travel or have telephones. It became almost impossible to find out what was going on around us. But somehow we heard some rumours about what was going on in Amsterdam. Maybe by mail. However, you were careful not to write too free. There was fear of interception. But what you could read between the lines was what counted, and for that, you had to know each other, or be aware of the circumstances.

We heard rumours that in Amsterdam Jews got letters from family or friends that had been transported. Those letters were telling their families that they were alright and working in camps. But somehow the family could tell that those letters were written under pressure and not true.

That could be done in some form of a family code.

For instance, they could refer and mention the name of some friend, who was known to be a liar. Or maybe mention an incident in their family life that actually never happened. That way the family became alerted and aware something was wrong.

But for a while those letters about the good camplife came in. That way the Nazis tried to take away the suspicion about the rumours that the Jews were killed in Poland or Germany.

And so there was less resistance for them to deal with.

The reality was so well screened and so impossible to imagine that it sometimes happened that some Jews had themselves captured in spite of a chance to hide out. Their hope was that they would go to the same camp as their family had been taken already. They hoped so much to see their family again.

Living in Utrecht, and in spite of disconnected phonelines, and the law that forbade the Jews to travel, we knew what happened in Amsterdam. We knew what had happened to some of our family that had been raided by the Nazis, and taken away.

My mother's youngest sister, Elizabeth, was raided in her second-floor apartment and shoved down the stairs. She had a deadly heart attack in the street.

My Uncle Salle, my mother's brother, when he got raided started to sing loud when he came outside in the street. It was an old well-known streetsong. Everybody thought he had become insane.

But Salle singing a common streetsong, while his life was in danger, was not crazy, and not out of character. He always had a reason.

I remembered the words to that streetsong, which were:
We are not going home yet
not for a long time
not for a long time.

I realized that he probably tried to give other Jews some message, a warning. And taunt the Nazis. He must have had a reason.

Juda, about twenty-three, the oldest son of Elizabeth, got arrested for possession of explosive chemicals. Juda insisted they were not his, that somebody planted on him. But it gave the Nazis an excuse to kill him.

Rumours about the raids when the Nazis came with their trucks and the Jews had to stay in their houses, waiting to be taken.

And rumours about Jews trying to escape from rooftops.

The Jewhunters knew there was no escape from there.

And then . . . ?

***

Now it became a serious matter to look for a place to escape to or hide out. And we were a big family.

Pa had met somebody whom he knew from the store. That man told him the name of somebody else who might know somebody who might be willing to help.

And so contact was made.

There had been a long discussion before we knew what to do or where we could place our babies. There might have been somebody who wanted to look after one of our babies. There was a single woman who was very insisting and demanding to have one of our little boys. Max and Bram were against it.

They hoped that they would be taken up in a family with other children.

But they found nobody. And then we heard, maybe from Pa, that Bram and me and the children might be able to be together somewhere. Maybe Pa or maybe Max might have contacted somebody from the underground.

The underground was just beginning for themselves trying to find out whom they could trust.

Life was tense for those people who were involved.

For the majority, who were ignorant or did not want to know, life went on.

While we were afraid for our lives, our neighbour complained to Mom that the tea ration upset her because she did not have enough to enjoy her everyday afternoon teatime!

And while we were denied to have our business and denied money to buy groceries, and while we were living in fear, my mother gave a package of the scarce tea to her neighbour so that she could enjoy her regular afternoon tea.

Then a woman we did not know came and wanted my weddinggown, because, she said, "I would have never use for it anymore." Somebody, Max probably, politely told the human vulture that she had to wait. That I was (still) living.

21

Walking Away from Home

There was danger in the atmosphere. We felt there was no more time left for us. It was urgent to leave.

We had to leave. We knew that, or thought we knew that. But we did not realise that we had to leave everything behind and just go out of the frontdoor, trying to save our lives. That we would be separated. That we never could come back.

Just start walking. Walk out of our home. Walk away from our family. Walk away from our livingroom where we ate, and our bed where we went to sleep.

Walk away from each other . . .

Then, at some day, at some moment, we started to walk.

First Pa and Mom.

They took off the yellow Davidsstar and were escorted to a home where they would be hiding out. To their astonishment their guide was a little boy of twelve years old. Pa asked him if he knew what he was doing. The boy, Jaap Gerritse was his name, answered with a short yes. Pa asked him if he was not afraid. Jaap answered, "No, I am praying to God and He will lead us safely to our home."

And there is where Pa and Mom went. To the family Gerritse.

Pa and Mom had left behind their family and their homelife. They just had to walk away from what they loved.

They just had to walk away.

We had not been told where Pa and Mom were going. Not knowing where the "underdivers" (civilians in hiding) were prevented betrayal under torture in case someone was taken prisoner. The underground knew contacts.

Then Bram and I walked out with our children. Bram had received an address where we should go to.

And Bram brought us there.

The family Priem was a labourer's family. Man, wife, and a few young children.

Max was the last one.

I imagine him walking through our home. Through the rooms. Looking at some things. Touching some things. Looking at the beds in which our babies had slept. Also making sure that we had nothing left that could have betrayed us.

What were his thoughts? Did he know this was the end? The end of our homelife and the end of our family? Did he feel it was the last moment of a lifestyle? Being there left alone, did he already feel the hopelessness and loss?

He turned to our closet, opening it wide. Taking out my pure white satin bridal gown. He might have looked at it once more.

And then he tore it apart!

Then Max walked away.

Adieu Max, thank you.

Max went into hiding. Max the quiet man. Full of good feelings, but also a good insight into what was happening. Later on, we found out how he did his share in the resistance, to fight a massacre he felt was going on, without anybody knowing facts.

Or maybe he knew.

Max, my brother.

And then? The Nazis came. Maybe the same day. We had not escaped a minute too soon. Or else how did they know so fast?

The Nazis sealed the house.

We heard a rumour that a day later one seal was broken. Had Max gone back? Had the neighbours been stealing?

Then all seals were broken and the human vultures came. Looting, plundering, robbing. Nazis and others. They were in our home. They took our clothes, our babyblankets. They took our cups and saucers. We would never drink from them again. They took our silver spoons and forks. We would never eat from them again.

Part of our silver and jewellery had been placed with neighbours or friends, for safekeeping.

We had nice things.

But we never saw it again.

They took our furniture. Things that our family had carefully chosen and really liked. It had surrounded us and meant "home" to us for many years. We would never use it again. It was all taken. We could never return. We knew, and felt hunted. We had lost our home. Our family was separated.

We had stopped to exist. Our way of life had been destroyed.

Maybe we did not yet fully realise it then, but our family would never be together again.

22

Trying to Adjust

Bram and me and our babies were in the house of the labourer and his family. We got a room, and Bram and the babies stayed there always. Out of sight. I became the cleaning lady and did all the woman's dirty diaper washing and other cleaningwork. This way my presence there could be explained. A cleaning lady for a poor labourer family who had three children of their own was not a very good pretence.

But it had to do.

Bram right away made sure that he paid them very well for their room and board, so that in that way they might feel slightly more comfortable.

We were very worried about our little boys. Their being there could not be explained, and thus they could not show themselves. Also, they should not be heard. If they played or cried it meant that if the family had company, that would betray us all.

It is hard for two little boys to be quiet in one room all day. Day after day. For weeks. For months. For how long?

Bram and I had a double bed, and during most of the day Leo and Jack had to stay in that bed, so no footsteps would be heard.

They had to eat and play there. At night they went to their own bed, which was smaller.

Even now I am proud that they were the most beautiful and well looked after babies anybody had ever seen. We got one kettle of warm water a day. Not really every day. But the bottles were warmed up somehow, the babies were bathed and had clean clothes every day, and their hair was shiny and curly.

The woman of the house said: "Your babies, in your bad circumstances, look like princes compared to mine. You are another class of people."

For a moment I was worried. Our family hiding out with a jealous mother did not seem safe. But we could not change anything. We had to ignore it.

It was a cold winter, and Bram and I bathed in icy water. But we became easily used to that.

Thinking about the Nazi alternative made us accept everything.

After we were there a while, we noticed that Jack started to look very pale and sick. He was so very young and had never been outside. He did not seem to feel well. He needed a doctor's attention. Our Jewish doctor was not available anymore, and we did not know anyone else who could be trusted.

I don't know with whom Bram made contact, but via the underground, who knew a reliable one, a doctor came to see Jack. He told us that Jack needed sun. But it was impossible for us to give him that. Jack could not go outside and we could not go outside. We felt helpless.

But that doctor arranged for Jack to be for a few weeks at the home of a nurse, who looked after him, and gave him sunlamp treatments every day.

That doctor was also impressed how we kept up and said he would like to come back to visit and for some talking and company. That sounded so nice. But we all understood that it really would be too dangerous.

We never knew the name of that doctor, because names were never mentioned in those circumstances.

The nurse kept him some weeks, till we finally became worried and wanted Jack back.

When Jack came back, he had a beautiful suntan. And he was wearing a new pretty sweater and had a toy in his hand.

Thinking back, you realize that the underground were not only fighting.

They were also real people.

Max had been hiding out somewhere for a while. We never knew where. But we were told he did dangerous things. Probably by Mrs. Gerritse, who was our contact. We were told that Max was outside after curfew till deep in the night. Nobody mentioned anything, but after the war we found out he had fought in the resistance. Probably sending and receiving Morse code communication from a transmitter and receiver he had built himself. And radios. As a soldier in the Dutch army he belonged to a special detail that was in charge of field communication.

Before he dived under, he had rented a little old house in the Keukenstraat in Utrecht. There he kept all kind of things we did not know of. Maybe radios, transmitters, weapons, or explosives. He knew about those things.

He did not want us to be involved or be endangered. But he asked Bram to keep paying the rent if anything happened to him.

I hope that the Nazis never found out about Max and that old house in the Keukenstraat.

After the war, some strange man that I vaguely remembered to have seen once before, recognised me while I was walking with Bram somewhere.

He came up to me and said: "Your brother Max was a respected man in the resistance. He did some important things. I want you to know that."

And before I realized it, the man had walked on and was out of sight.

I wish I knew more about Max and that man.

23

Betrayal . . .

We were hiding out. Living strictly indoors. Like in a prison. Waiting. For what?

Things on the outside turned for the worse. Proclamation after proclamation came out from the Germans. Any Dutchman who was hiding Jews would be punished and treated the same way as the Jews.

Then some shifting around happened. Our babies had to go to the family Gerritse, and my parents came to the family where we were. Max also went to Gerritse.

And the family Gerritse, whose house was now more of a halfway house, found a home for Jack with some neighbour.

Then it happened. Somebody had betrayed the Gerritses to the *Gestapo* (Ge-sta-po—Geheime Staatspolizei—Secret Police).

There was a raid. After a short heavy banging on the frontdoor, the Gestapo forced their way into the hall.

But before they started to go further into the house, and some of them were still in the hall, Mrs. Gerritse stalled for time.

Her shock and fear were genuine. But her mind worked at high level and fast.

So she explained to the Nazis that people were so suspicious and unfair, and that the sudden invasion of all those policemen confused her, and that her dinner that was on the stove was burning.

Would they mind if she went to the kitchen and looked after it?

No, they did not mind.

Mrs. Gerritse went to the kitchen and took from a little hiding place behind the coalstove a bag full of counterfeit identity papers and stolen ration cards.

And while the Gestapo still could hear her cry about her wasted food, she threw all evidence of illegal and anti-German activities on the red glowing coals! It was burned in a few minutes.

In the meantime, the son of Mrs. Gerritse, only twelve years old, handed Leo over the hedge to their neighbours. After that Max escaped.

Now Max came to Priem too.

And there we were. Pa and Mom, Max and Bram and me. Five Jews in the house of an unstable, unreliable, and afraid pair of Dutch people.

It was too much for them. One afternoon Priem came in and told us what he had done.

He had become scared and had gone to the Gestapo and told them that he had five Jews in the house, and he asked them to take us away.

Now his conscience bothered him and he told us about it to give us a chance to run.

The first thing we did was go into a little space under the stairs to hide out and try to find a way.

There we were, sitting huddled down because it was so small and we did not know what to do.

We were there and felt dehumanized. Robbed of dignity and full of fear. No panic. Just endless desperation.

Pa finally said: "Bram and Jet have to leave now and try to go under in the streets with other people. Just go. We will stay here and await our fate."

Max said: "I go too."

And Pa said, "No, Max, you look Jewish. People might know you, and then you endanger the kids. You stay with us and share our fate as the family we are."

And Max said: "All right, Pa."

So Pa and Mom and Max stayed behind. And when we were leaving, I kissed Mom and maybe Pa and Max. Then Mom cried out: "I will never see you again." Pa said to Mom, "Quiet, Clara."

Mom was quiet. So was Max. All looked strange, pale.

And so Pa and Mom and Max chose to stay behind and let us have a chance on life.

No heroism, but parents and a brother who were loving and gave their lives for the ones they loved. Our babies and us.

My God, we left them. It had to be. We had two babies to care for. I have no guilt feelings. But I feel so sad, especially for Max, who never had a chance for a life of his own.

It must have left scars on the hearts of Bram and me. Because afterwards, Bram and I could never smile anymore.

Again we started walking. Away from our family.

Mom had been right, when she had cried out.

We never saw each other again . . .

***

Much later, we heard that they had been taken from another address. I don't know where and I am not sure.

Bram and I walked into the streets. Without our yellow Davidsstar, which in itself was a crime.

There we were walking and felt abandoned. All other people lived in homes and had a bed to go to. We were in the streets and in danger. All we wanted was to be part of a life that had a light on in their livingrooms, which made it look so good and safe.

But we had no home, no bed, and no livingroom. And we were afraid for our lives.

Where could we go?

Bram finally said: "Let us go to Tilburg, where I know a family who are anti-Nazi."

We went by train to Tilburg.

Bram found that family and we could stay there for a few days.

Right away Bram tried to find out what had happened to our young sons.

I don't know how he found out, maybe he had contacted Mrs. Gerritse, but he told me: "Jet, our children have been betrayed and taken away by the Gestapo and sent to Amsterdam. I go to Amsterdam."

In Amsterdam, Bram went to Uncle Simon, Pa's youngest brother. He was still around because he had bought some time, bribing the Nazis with handfuls of diamonds.

In Amsterdam there seemed to be a little group who had found a special channel, some Nazis who could be bribed with diamonds.

In return, the Nazis gave them a stamp with a certain number which coded them for later transports.

When finally, later, Uncle Simon and his pretty Portuguese Jewish wife, Aunt Marie, were taken by the Gestapo, Aunt Marie was dressed in an elegant skirt suit. The buttons of the suit were covered with the same fabric as the suit and looked chic. But under the fabric, within every button, a diamond had been sewn in.

But now Simon was still there and he brought Bram to a building where all children were concentrated, before deportation to a deathcamp.

For children there was no other destination.

But I heard that later.

Bram went into the building alone and spoke there to the man in charge, Dr. Susskind. The doctor, a Jew himself, promised Bram that when the next transport would go, he would hold back Leo and Jack, and then give them back to Bram. But until then he could do nothing.

Bram came back to Tilburg and told me that.

Bram also told me that he had heard from Simon that my parents and Max had been transported to concentration camp Westerbork.

But before they had to leave the police station in Utrecht, my parents "persuaded" (bribed) a policeman to warn Selma, Bram's sister, to leave the place where she was hiding, because the police knew it. But Selma did not want to go. She thought if she would be taken that she had a chance to go to the same camp as her family and meet them there. Nobody could imagine the truth.

My family, even in their own despair, thought of helping others.

I could not absorb it all. My parents and Max and our children, all in hands of the Nazis. My mind did not even understand the real meaning of it all.

Suddenly, I shouted and cried, and could not stop. I just tried to drive it away by shouting. Until I was too tired.

A day later, I sent Mom a new dress of mine that had been made of warm woollen coat fabric. Bram sent Pa a German medicine to inhale for his asthma. I realize now, and it hurts me, that we did not send Max anything.

Our family smuggled a note out of the camp to acknowledge receipt of it and thanked us.

One or two days went by. Suddenly Bram said to me: "Jet, I have no rest, I go back to Amsterdam."

God must have given him that feeling because that day a transport was going. And Leo and Jack were going to be on it.

In front of the building where the children were, was a Nazi standing on guard. I knew how much fear a Nazi uniform could give. The men in those uniforms had power over any Jew if they discovered one.

Bram was determined to go inside the building and save our sons. That was his only thought. He must have gathered his mental strength. He behaved with an appearance of authority. That was part of him.

Then Bram, with the display of that authority, pushed the guard away, went inside to Dr. Susskind, and demanded our children back.

Dr. Susskind let Bram go to the backyard, and there a nurse handed Bram three children. Our own two sons and a pretty little girl. After the war the grandmother of the little girl was found. She did not know that her granddaughter had been saved.

It is natural that a father wants to save his sons.

But, still, this needed intelligence and courage.

Jack went to Utrecht to the family van Brummelen, who named him Pim. Many years after the war we still called him Pim.

Bram brought Leo to me in Tilburg. Leo was very skinny and behaved very frightened. What had happened to our babies? I could not ask. They were so young and small. What had they experienced? I could not even be for a moment out of Leo's sight or he cried desperately. It was heartbreaking.

And he ate so much. They must have hungered. He never had enough, and I was feeding him white bread cubes with butter and sugar. All day long.

Also, all the new and good quality clothes and their luggage had disappeared. He wore strange clothes. But we ignored that at that time.

After a few short days, a home for Leo had to be found, because we could not stay with that family in Tilburg.

Somehow, Bram made contact with the underground and Leo would go to a home.

But we did not know where.

And then Bram and I had to leave.

We had walked around without the yellow Davidsstar, but it was obvious we did not belong there.

Bram realised that, and after some thinking, he said: "Jet, I don't know what to do here. Maybe I should go to Zwolle. I know there an old English teacher of mine who probably is reliable and maybe helpful."

That was taking a risk.

Because it was a minority of the Dutch people that was connected with the resistance or with the hiding out of Jews. So you had in the first place to find out who you could trust and who had connections with the underground. It was a dangerous thing just to approach somebody and find out how reliable they were. You relied on acquaintances from before the war or you observed someone you thought maybe was not antisemitic, but was just pro-Nazi. It was a limited choice, and it was always a chance you took.

But Bram decided to go alone to Zwolle and contact his English teacher.

When Bram came back to me in Tilburg, he told me that his teacher had contacted someone he knew and then said we should go to Hattem. We were told to walk together on a certain country road, and we would be recognized by somebody who would meet us there. And we should follow him.

We left Tilburg and we went to Hattem. We were walking on that country road. It was a quiet road with trees and some houses. We walked in the middle of the road. Slowly.

It was evening and it got darker. We felt very lonely and strange, not knowing what was going to happen to us. Maybe we were walking into a trap? We felt afraid.

Finally, a well-dressed man came walking up to us and sort of made sure who we were. He started walking beside Bram. We were quiet. He took us to his house.

And there we met Mrs. van Binsbergen.

24

Hiding Out

The family van Binsbergen consisted of him, a notary public, Mrs. van Binsbergen, a former schoolteacher, four children, a maid by the name of Pleuntje, and two hunting dogs.

They lived on a country road in a nice house surrounded by a big yard.

Their neighbours on one side were a pot and pan manufacturer. He was Jewish, but his wife was not Jewish and from Swiss origin. Because of his Swiss wife, he was allowed to stay in his house.

On the other side lived somebody who was somehow connected with parliament.

Van Binsbergen told us right away that we had to change our names into non-Jewish ones. So Bram became Henk and Jet became Jo.

Then we were shown our duties. Helping to clean, peel potatoes, making the beds, and mending socks. When Bram asked how much we had to pay weekly, van Binsbergen said he did not want any money. But when Bram insisted, he accepted a fair weekly amount so that everybody would feel comfortable. Besides money, Bram had from Pa some old gold, broken gold watches, pieces of gold chains, and bracelets. Van Binsbergen sold it for us gradually, whenever we needed cash. He was surprised about the prices he could get for it.

During the day, if it was possible, we sat upstairs in a guestroom. At nighttime, or if there were visitors in the house, we had to go to our hiding place.

The hiding place was above their livingroom hearth, and it was only a meter high and a few meters long. So all we could do there was lie down. If they had company in the livingroom it became almost unbearable not to move or sneeze or just change position.

We could enter it from the bathroom upstairs, and there were some planks to move to go in, and to put them back when we were in. There might have been a piece of carpet on it to camouflage the entrance.

When we were there a few days, Bram realized there was a food problem. We did not exist officially and had no ration cards.

Bram contacted Mrs. Gerritse in Utrecht. And Mrs. Gerritse herself came to Hattem with ration cards for us. Mrs. Gerritse also provided us with a false ID card in the name of Wickevoort. Everybody was obliged to show their ID card on command to any Nazi who asked for it. The name Wijnberg would have been too Jewish.

This seems all very simple but was in fact quite a complicated operation. It was not only the Jews that needed food ration cards. There were also underground fighters. Besides the food ration cards, there were new ID cards needed for saboteurs and Jews. Or sometimes the J was removed from the Jewish ID cards.

For all those things there was an organization set up, that specialized in counterfeit papers. They obtained the floorplans of the official distribution offices and stole, raided or robbed them. There was a lot involved and it was very dangerous for everybody. Anyone who was connected with it and got caught, had the certainty to be tortured. The torture was a sure means for the Gestapo to obtain names and addresses which would lead them to others.

This, and other information we got from Mrs. Gerritse. Also that the resistance had started to send and receive coded messages with England. And that there were hidden printing presses that printed an underground socialistic newspaper. The "Free People" was the name of that paper. Bram wanted to be part of that group. But Mrs. Gerritse was against it. Because it was not practical in his hidden position.

On the surface everything seemed to be settled now. But not for long.

One day Bram and I were called downstairs in the livingroom.

Mr. and Mrs. van Binsbergen were sitting there and we were standing there. They told us that they were informed that Pa and Mom and Max had been taken by the Gestapo from concentrationcamp Westerbork and sent away to an unknown destination.

They handed Bram some letters, meant for Bram and me, that had been smuggled out of concentrationcamp Westerbork. Also a letter that had been addressed to Uncle Simon.

Pa warned us to be careful. He wrote in his letter to us that his bookkeeper had money from him for safekeeping, and if we needed any, Bram could go there and ask for it. If that was not possible, then he had written his brother Simon to give us what we needed. The money that they had carried themselves with them had been confiscated.

Pa also wrote that they had been taken from another address than where we had left them. Again some money seemed to have "disappeared." Now they had no money at all with them anymore. He had tried to tell the Nazis that we were not all Jewish and to let them free. This was not true of course, but was maybe an opening move to a bribe. Without success.

Finally, Pa wrote to say that he accepted fate and that they probably would be on transport with the next train. It would be, maybe on his birthday.

27 June 1943...

Mom wrote about her fear for our babies. She wrote in a form of code that I could understand, but would give others the idea that she wrote about some children of friends, that were sick. In case the letters come in wrong hands, that should prevent to identify the children as Jewish and family. She was still protecting her family from that concentration camp. She knew that the addresses had been betrayed to the police.

They did not know for sure that Bram had saved them. But Mom wrote to us: "You have duties and take care of your children, and each other." She wrote: "You go on, live, till we are together again."

Max also wrote, in some form of code, to give us information without giving outsiders the meaning behind it. He wrote about the traitor who in his presence told the police where our little boys were. And how it had sickened him. And in code, he gave us the name of the police inspector. He wanted us to know it. And that the same police inspector had taken Mom's purse with quite an amount of money.

Max also wrote names of many prominent people we knew and that he met them now that they were also prisoners in the camp. Max warned me to behave stronger. And carry on. Max, my big brother.

His last wish to us was the Hebrew command:

"Chazak we Ematz!"
Be strong and courageous!

But not my father or mother or Max complained about their fate. They knew they would be deported with the next train. But each of them tried to give us strength and hope for the future. "Be careful. Till we are together again. Chazak we Ematz!" Be strong and courageous!

I started to cry, and Bram was worried that I would get hysterical and upset our hosts and maybe endanger us. So he said right away something like: "Be quiet, Jet." He might have held my hand. And so we stood there, and I did not cry.

For twenty years I could never cry for my parents or my brother.

But I cried for anything else.

And I had them always on my mind for all those years.

25

The Trains

The resistance fighters in Holland were active. But it was a minority. The average Dutchman was uninvolved and went on as usual. That could be understood. But we did not understand the train engineers who drove the Jews away in cattle-wagons. Hiding out, without communication, we did not know the full truth what was happening.

We just hoped, and prayed, that the engineers would refuse to drive the trains, go on strike before it was too late for our family. That they would stop and make an end to the taking away of families and children to a fate unknown to us.

There was no information about their destination and we were afraid. It was only much later that we heard the facts.

Those engineers brought the cattlewagons with their locked-in, suffering people—grandparents, children, young men, and babies—from Holland to their death destinations. Locked in those cattlecars without food or drink or relief.

They were running those trains for days at a time, knowing the contents. They still went on for years.

It only became different when English fighter planes started to shoot at the engineers from the Dutch railways because they wanted to disrupt all general transportation to Germany. Because trains brought clothes, food, and war supplies to Germany. Then, and only then, the engineers stayed away. Because they themselves felt threatened.

Why did the English wait so long? Why did the engineers not strike sooner?

It was too late for the Dutch Jewish people.

It was too late for our family.

Too late...

Too late!

26

Were Our Children Safe?

We began to feel more alone. The slight hope that we might have had that our family was maybe somewhere was leaving us.

From now on we were on our own. Two young people with two young children, living a kind of life for which we had not been prepared.

Hiding out from deadly enemies, no homelife, our children separated from us, and waiting for the war to end to find out about our standing in life, with or without family around us.

We could not feel sure about anything.

Once more, Mrs. Gerritse came from Utrecht to bring our food ration cards. This time she had with her a picture from Jack. She told us that while Jack was hiding out with the family van Brummelen, they had also for a short time a Jewish girl from Zwolle that knew Bram, but did not know whether he had children. When she the first time saw Jack, she became all excited and said: "That is Bram Wijnberg's son." She had never seen Jack before and had no way of connecting Bram with Jack. But she was positive. When we heard about that we were surprised and a little worried. If she could identify Jack, we just hoped nobody else could. It was unusual how she could recognize him so positive while she did not even know of his birth.

Somehow it worried me.

The picture Mrs. Gerritse had given Bram looked as if one side of it had been cut off with a scissor.

Bram asked Mrs. Gerritse if she also had a picture of Leo.

Then Mrs. Gerritse explained that Jack and Leo both had been on that picture, but Leo's picture was not so clear, and therefore they had cut it off.

I believed her and just felt unhappy that there was no picture from Leo. I would not have minded if it had been blurred, I would have recognized him anyway.

But Bram was always more alert. After Mrs. Gerritse left, Bram told me he had doubts. He said, "We actually don't know where Leo is, and we really don't have proof that Leo was on that picture."

Bram said: "I want to know. And because nobody tells us, we have to find out for ourselves. Come on, let us go!"

We just put our coats on and wanted to leave. While going downstairs, van Binsbergen saw us, and asked us what we were doing with our coats on. We had never before left the house. Bram told him that we were leaving, and why.

Van Binsbergen seemed shocked and told Bram: "You cannot go out just like that. It is suicide! Stay here, and I will go and find out for you. I know a student priest who is connected with the underground. I will ask him if he knows or can find out about your son. I'm going right now."

And he did.

When he came back, he told us that the priest would have to search around carefully and that it might take a few weeks before he could know.

About ten days later we noticed that van Binsbergen had a visitor. When the visitor had left, van Binsbergen told us that it had been the priest who had come to report to him. Suddenly I felt weak from fear.

But van Binsbergen went on and told us that a group of Jewish babies, and maybe some older children, had been smuggled to Friesland, and that Leo had been one of them.

Following that lead, the student priest had found Leo on the farm of Obbe and Marie Faber. Obbe and Marie thought that Leo's parents had been killed, and had adopted him, giving him their family name: Uppie Faber.

But we just could not believe it. We needed proof. We wanted to see Leo. Then, to reassure us, they arranged a meeting with Obbe and Marie at the van Binsbergens'.

Obbe and Marie came from Friesland for a visit, and brought Leo with them. And while they were with us, we could not keep our eyes away from Leo. But he did not recognize us and acted shy. I wanted to cuddle him, but he walked away. Still, we were happy and satisfied. He looked good. Bram and I felt better since we really had seen him.

A few weeks later, when there was some natural sheep-swool available, I asked Mrs. van Binsbergen to buy some for me. Then I knitted for Leo and Jack the nicest, strongest, and warmest little jackets. And then I embroidered them.

When Obbe and Marie received Leo from the underground, they had no name for him, and they thought his parents had been taken and did not live anymore. While I had the very best in clothes packed for our children, Leo was in rags. All his own clothes had been stolen. Obbe and Marie did not have any idea what his background could have been, but from his appearance it did not look good.

But a Jewish woman that was hiding with them temporarily had another opinion. She noticed that, for a toddler, Leo was eating very neat. That he was obviously trained and remained dry. Even at night in bed. And when he got better clothes from Marie, he kept himself clean. She came to the true conclusion that the dirty rags that Leo had arrived in did not have anything to do with the child's background, which must have been quite good.

27

An Unreliable Nephew

Time went by. Winter had come to an end and was followed by spring. We did not count days or months. We kept track of the seasons. There were rumours that the war would not take long anymore. But we realized that were just the kind of rumours a war creates. Especially in spring. From an upstairs window, but slightly away from it so nobody could see us from the outside, we looked into the garden.

Near the window was a tree in which a couple of birds were building a nest. We followed their efforts and felt good when we saw them return to their little home with little twigs to make it stronger, and little feathers that would make it soft and warm. We were thinking about our own destroyed homelife, and it gave us the feeling that we also wanted to make a cozy home for ourselves, and Leo and Jack, our children.

We had been married a few years now and never had a feeling of home and rest.

Better not think about that.

When the eggs in the nest turned into little birds, we admired the hard work of the old birds in feeding them.

When would we have our family in a home of our own? How long would this war go on?

We had to wait and wait.

And while the war continued, we had to keep on hiding out. And the longer it lasted, the more difficult the situations that came up and had to be dealt with.

Suddenly a new problem appeared, from an unsuspected source.

Somehow, there were in the van Binsbergen's family a few that knew that he was hiding Jews. One of them was a young nephew of about eighteen years old. He was an unstable fellow who did not do too well in school or anything else.

So, like many of that kind, he joined the NSB. They hoped to make themselves impressive by wearing a uniform and boots, and get some money out of it as well.

One day, he came to visit his uncle and aunt, where we were hiding out. When he came, we had to go to our hiding place, which was right above the livingroom, and from where we could hear most of what was spoken there.

He came in the afternoon before van Binsbergen was back from his office.

When finally van Binsbergen came home, he greeted his nephew pleasantly and asked him what he was doing.

And then the nephew started to explain that he was a member of a group of young Nazi sympathizers and that he had heard that his uncle was hiding out Jews.

He warned his uncle to get rid of the Jews and to pay him an amount of money so he would not talk about it.

Otherwise, he would inform about the Jews and that would expose his uncle.

Van Binsbergen listened quietly. Then, just as quietly, started to explain to his nephew that he also was part of a group. But this group was anti-Nazi and anti-collaborators.

That this group, within the underground, had a house somewhere in the country, and whenever there was somebody that posed a danger to them, that person was made a prisoner and put in that house. If they were still difficult somehow, they disappeared from that house and nobody heard from them again. He hoped that his nephew understood what he was trying to say.

To make sure, however, van Binsbergen grabbed his nephew, and with his bare hands systematically beat him up. We could hear the thud of the blows.

After he stopped beating his nephew, van Binsbergen, still acting calm, warned his nephew that if anything happened to himself, his family, or the Jews, that house in the country was waiting for him, and the underground fighters would be deciding what they would do with him.

Then he let his nephew go.

But to make sure that his family knew the seriousness of his threat, he told the parents of the boy to keep a strict control on their son and his Nazi ambitions, if they wanted to keep him alive.

If van Binsbergen had to make the choice between the life of his nephew, or the life and safety of his wife and children, it was obvious what he would do.

Van Binsbergen had his priorities.

28

A Reason for Living

We were living. But we were hiding out and could not do what is normal in everyday life.

No business to attend to for Bram, no cooking or household for me. We could not even think or plan. Our thoughts were completely taken over by our fears. The fears and worries for our children, the fear of capture.

Bram tried to follow whatever news he heard about the war and had a good insight into politics and what was happening. He made logical conclusions about what to expect from the German or Allied armies. We also talked a lot about food and what we would like to eat if we ever could choose again.

Of course, this was not enough to fill our days. And we tried to read if we found anything around with words on it. And maybe by lack of stimulation or purpose, maybe because we lived in a form of vacuum, out of touch, I don't know. Maybe because there was nothing else available to us, but we became interested in teenage stories and later even went down to books for grade one and grade two children's books. Maybe our isolation was the cause of it. Or the fear for the life of our children, the sadness over the loss of our family. And also our fear for our own existence and future might have forced everything else out.

Once, we stood in the upstairs bathroom and looked down from the window. We considered our chances, if we were high enough, to be killed if we would jump out. No, maybe just broken bones and a chance of lifelong damage. Not high enough to die from it. We had our babies to care for too. We did not say anything. Bram and I, standing together, thinking and feeling the same, speaking was not necessary.

We just turned our back to the window, to go on with our waiting and our fears.

And the realization that we would not abandon our children in this world, and leave them behind, separated from each other and loose from their roots.

29

Needing a Doctor

While the war went on, meat became scarcer. The rations were very low. Then against all threats, rules, and orders from the Nazis, people started to buy from the black market.

Farmers sold their meat clandestine, at high prices, without asking for ration coupons. But only to people they knew or trusted.

One day, van Binsbergen came home with half a pig in the trunk of his car. From the black market. But when he had it in the house, there was a problem. You cannot cook half a pig.

Then Bram, who had apprenticed for a while with a Jewish butcher, offered to cut it up in steaks, chops, and whatever else was possible.

That saved the day. From then on, we got every day pork with our meal.

I was very hungry, but could not eat it. I had never eaten pork before. But that did not explain why the smell of preparing it made me so terribly nauseated. And then, a worry we already had became a certainty.

I was pregnant again! We became frightened. What to do?

It would be dangerous for the family van Binsbergen to have our baby born there. It would be a complete giveaway for them and us. Going away from there, and to risk it on the outside, was also a terrible risk. What if we were recognized by friends, or enemies? What would happen to a pregnant Jewish woman if she fell in hands of the Gestapo?

The more we thought about it, the more afraid we became. We decided not to say anything until I could not hide it anymore. That took until I was five and a half months. Bram and I, we agreed that we would take the only chance we saw, and that was to leave. We did not want to endanger the van Binsbergens.

Finally, we asked for a conversation with Mr. and Mrs. van Binsbergen. Bram told them that we were leaving, and why. And again, the van Binsbergens showed their high human quality. They wanted us to stay! And they would arrange another home for me when my time was there.

My nausea in the meantime became a problem. I just could not eat, which might affect the baby. I needed a doctor. But which doctor could we trust? It had to be a doctor who would not betray us, or even talk about it. Then Bram remembered that one of the customers of their hotel, a farmer himself, had a brother who was a doctor in Hattem. The name was van Haringen.

So Bram and I, for the very first time in one and a half years, had to go out and try to speak to that doctor.

We waited till it was dark. When we came there Bram rang the bell. The maid opened the door. Bram told the maid that I was sick and asked if the doctor was in.

"Yes, and will you go to the office, please."

When the doctor came, he asked us routinely our name and address. Then Bram told him that we were Jewish and that we had no address. But that I needed help.

He almost threw us out! He shouted: "I don't know you and I don't want to know you. I have a regular practice and I don't want to have anything to do with illegal people."

Then Bram talked about his brother, the farmer, and reassured him we were not spies or provocateurs. That I was undernourished from nausea and that I was pregnant. Which he could see.

So he wrote in a hurry a prescription and sent us away.

The prescription helped.

30

Betrayed Again

Some things started to change.

Pleuntje, the maid of van Binsbergen, quit her job to work somewhere else. And then a new maid came.

We were observing her and trying to establish where her political sympathies were. We were watching for little telltale signs to find out her character, whether she could be relied on not to talk or maybe would be downright an informer. It was very important to be good at that, because giving your confidence to a stranger is risking your life and many others with it.

We never knew what happened, but after about six weeks, a car came rushing in the driveway. Van Binsbergens' neighbour (the Jewish manufacturer) jumped out, came running in the house, and warned Mrs. van Binsbergen that we were betrayed. A group of Green Police were on their bicycles from Zwolle on their way to Hattem to arrest us.

Then the neighbour ran away.

Mrs. van Binsbergen called us downstairs. She told us that the neighbour had warned her that the Nazis were on their way to take us away, and that the neighbour had advised Mrs. van Binsbergen to put us out of the house. Just put us both out of the door on the road. Without any other place to go to. Again, where could we go? Mrs. van Binsbergen did not want to do that.

We did not go to our hiding place. We just sat there and waited.

And then? How long did we wait? What did we think of? I don't know.

But to believe in God or not, to believe in miracles or not. Somebody or something acted for our lives. Because it started to rain, it started to pour, it started to hail and thunder. The Green Police on their bicycles decided to turn around and come back the next day!

In the meantime, van Binsbergen came home, put me in his car, and drove me to Uddel, where a cousin of his was a nurse. Bram contacted Pleuntje in her new job, and she arranged with the housekeeper and the lady of the house that Bram could hide out there.

And so Bram went in the night to the Castle in Wapenveld.

When the next day the Green Police came to van Binsbergen, he acted surprised. He told them they were mistaken about Jews, that he was a notary public, and if any of them wanted to make out their last will, he would be happy to do it for them!

Thinking about it now, it seems quite a coincidence that Pleuntje had left the van Binsbergens and went to a place where she later became the medium that provided an escape for Bram.

Coincidence?

31

Our Baby, the Nurse, and Me

Before Bram left for his new hiding address, van Binsbergen put me in his car. I was too dazed to realize anything. Mrs. van Binsbergen must have made sure I took some clothes with me. I could not think. Then van Binsbergen started the car and we left.

He drove fast through dark country roads. He did not talk. Just to say that we were going to a cousin of his family who was a visiting nurse on the old Crown domain in Uddel, near Apeldoorn. When we arrived there, I just had to go inside a small farmhouse where the nurse, Lien Voors, lived. And van Binsbergen had turned back and gone already. Not much was said, and I had to go to bed right away. For this small hamlet the bedtime was very early and I was too exhausted from everything that had happened.

Lien let me rest and a few days went by. She treated me like a favourite patient. About danger or hiding out she did not talk. She neglected the fact that she risked her life. It seemed that Lien, who had always lived alone there, without many people to talk with, did not mind having me as company.

Once, while she was preparing dinner, she asked me if I wanted to pick some blueberries for dessert. I just had to walk out of the door and I would find them growing under the bushes around the house. I stepped out and started to pick blueberries. But in my enthusiasm I went on picking and suddenly I was completely lost. I was surrounded by shoulder-high, goldcoloured grain for as far as I could see. I have no sense of direction and could not look for a farm or people because I was Jewish and illegal in Lien's house. I kept on walking, keeping myself low to be covered by the grain. I was afraid to meet people. I walked around and around for hours. Finally, I thought I maybe saw the house and walked up to it. I hoped it was Lien's house. When I came closer I recognized it and went in. Lien had been worried and I explained what had happened.

Then she told me, that in spite of those hours of walking, I had never been farther than ten minutes away from the house. But the ripe golden grain stood high and had hidden the small house.

Alida was born in August.

Harvest time.

Lien did her rounds on bicycle but came home often to check up on me. Then, one afternoon, I got some labourpains and Lien contacted the doctor she worked with.

I asked her if he was reliable for this situation and if he knew. She said it was OK.

Then a young doctor came and checked up on me. He said it would take some more time, and then he left, ignoring me completely. Maybe he was afraid to be too much involved.

When the pains kept going on, Lien again asked the doctor to come. He came back and looked me over, saw that things went too slow and that I just was too tired.

He said: "I will give you a needle that will speed it up." He did. Then things started to happen, and finally the baby came. A little girl. I thanked the doctor, he left, and I never heard or saw him again.

But then Lien took over. There seemed to be a nice little layette set for the baby. Lien enjoyed looking after her. She said it was such a pleasure to have a pretty and clean baby girl to look after. Different from the ones she handled on her rounds.

Our baby was named after Bram's mother, Alida, and after my mother, Clara. Bram and I wanted this so that our family names were to be continued.

I was nursing Alida myself and Lien made sure that I got the proper foods so I always had enough milk. Buttermilk porridge was the favourite food.

Lien was always with the baby at the very slightest noise she heard. Using as an excuse that I had to rest, she was tuned in on the baby night and day, ready to fuss over her.

For a while I had a backache that bothered me. After I started to feel better, I became homesick to be with Bram. Bram had to discuss that with the people where he was. It was quite a help that they agreed to take the baby and me. It was, after all, dangerous for them to hide Jews. When it was arranged that Alida and I would be leaving Lien, she had a snapshot made of herself in her nurse's uniform with my little baby in her arms. I might still have that picture.

So our baby was born while running away from the Nazis. And now I want to thank Lien Voors, visiting nurse on a bicycle.

Courageous woman.

32

The Castle in Wapenveld

After I had left the home of van Binsbergen, Bram left and tried to find his new hiding address. The Castle in Wapenveld was not really a castle, but a big old house, surrounded with grounds the size of a park. It was owned by an old lady, Mrs. Straub, who had lived there with her husband and her household staff for many years.

Now she lived there alone and had a housekeeper-companion, Mrs. Underhill, the maid Pleuntje, and a man who looked after the park grounds.

That man lived rentfree in a house belonging to the old lady, Mrs. Straub.

And here, to the Castle, came Bram, by means of Pleuntje, the former maid of van Binsbergen. Pleuntje had influenced Mrs. Underhill, the housekeeper, and she in turn had put it to the old lady.

Bram got a room upstairs.

When Alida was born in Uddel, I sent somehow the news to Bram. Maybe via Lien Voors and van Binsbergen.

Bram answered and wrote he was all right. But again, we lived separated. Bram in Wapenveld alone, and I was in Uddel with our baby.

I wanted Bram to see our little daughter. We became homesick for each other and wanted to be together.

After a while, and some persuasion from Mrs. Underhill and Pleuntje, Mrs. Straub agreed to take me in too, with the baby. They understood that we needed to be together, and there were even arrangements made for transportation. It was risky to go by train, but somehow there was a car to bring the baby and me.

Maybe the underground was helping out. Maybe via van Binsbergen.

After I was half a day at the Castle, we suddenly faced a new kind of problem. It had become impossible for me to hide out. The baby would cry, and the baby needed milk, and the diapers had to be washed and hung up to dry.

Then Bram had the ingenious idea that I should go under the pretence of a Rotterdam woman whose house had been bombed and whose husband was working in Germany. This way Bram could stay in hiding and I could look after our baby.

A while before, Mrs. Gerritse had provided us with counterfeit or stolen *Ausweis* (ID cards) in the name of Wickevoort. But, pretending we had been bombed out, I could say I had lost my papers and so maybe could avoid showing them.

It was dangerous. I could not afford to make a mistake. But there was no choice!

Then I was introduced to the old lady, Mrs. Straub.

She was a frail, grey haired lady, who was between seventy-eight and eighty years old, I guessed. She did not speak well anymore and was difficult to understand. But she was extremely alert, intelligent, and educated. She seemed to find me acceptable. Somehow, Mrs. Straub had noticed that Bram, besides Dutch, also could speak French, German, and English. Then she appointed Bram to come to her livingroom every day for some hours and read aloud from her books in any of those languages. She had a big library!

Also, in the evening Mrs. Underhill and Bram and I were "asked" to play bridge with her. And when she felt good, Bram and I were invited to eat with her in the diningroom. She apologised that her eating manners had deteriorated while she became older.

She liked to see the baby and it became a habit that every day, after Lida had her bath, that I walked by with her and exchanged a few words with Mrs. Straub. She enjoyed looking at our little girl. I feel that it was good that Bram was reading for her and that she accepted Lida and me. She was a nice lady. She had been married to some professor in astronomy, and they never had children.

Later in the day, when she went for her daily walk in her own park, I had to accompany her. That helped her housekeeper-companion, Mrs. Underhill.

Not far from Wapenveld, the German army had a garrison with anti-aircraft weapons. When the English bombers were flying over on their way to Germany, there was often shooting from both sides.

And then the shards were coming down as a dangerous rain.

Bram went sometimes to a hidden part on the roof because it gave him a good feeling to see hundreds and hundreds of those English planes on their way to their targets in Germany. Bridges, dams, munitions storage, and similar war objects. When flying over, those bomber planes made a heavy droning sound. They were a solid force.

Often Bram came downstairs with a piece of metal that had been part of a bullet or grenade that the Germans and English were shooting at each other. Bram was in danger to get hit by it, and we all asked him not to go to the roof anymore and take chances.

When Bram did not go to the roof, we stood somewhere together and we both looked.

It was an impressive sight. High up in the sky, hundreds and hundreds of those bomberplanes, flying in solid and correct formations, leaving behind long white smoke stripes in the air and making a heavy droning sound. In order to confuse and misdirect the radar that was used to locate them as a target for German anti-aircraft shooting, they threw out millions and millions of light metal strips.

It was an unbelievable sight. All those planes, the white smoke stripes behind them, high against the sky. The heavy droning sound. And under and around them, millions and millions of silvery strips whirling out of the sky, creating shining clouds around them. Never before or again have I seen anything so grand and so fascinating.

It was as if the sky had opened up and gave a show.

It was a war show, a show of strength, and the intelligence behind this gave us some confidence. But still, it was a war show.

Mrs. Straub was a really old lady. But she was quite active, intelligent, and had a sharp tongue. She used to make every day a walk in her own park accompanied by Mrs. Underhill. When English planes flew over, there was shooting, but Mrs. Straub insisted on her daily walk. Shooting or no shooting.

One day she was very dressed up for her walk and had added some colour to her outfit. She was wearing some ribbon on her coat, in the colours from the Dutch flag: red, white, and blue. And on her hat, very visible, a bright-orange corsage, the Dutch royal colour, to express "Oranje boven" ("Orange on Top"), support for the Royal House. When we looked at her, she asked, almost arrogant: "Don't you know it is our queen's birthday today?"

I was slightly terrified, and hoped she would walk in the middle of the park where nobody could see us from the road. I could not afford that she drew that kind of attention. I guess for my sake she stayed out of sight.

While all food was rationed, Mrs. Straub fed a little dog she had, most of her own food. And while food was scarce, this dog was horribly fat. We all ignored the animal, except Pleuntje. She disliked the little fat and lazy dog, and she said she was going to teach him to walk up the stairs. She put him on the stairs and walked behind him to push him up the next step. It did not work and Pleuntje became disgusted and gave up. It was funny, but we understood Pleuntje's anger. While food was scarce for children and people, this little dog was outrageous.

But after this little exercise we all forgot about it.

Pleuntje too.

33

Bram Standing Invisible

It was not impossible for our family to act as gentile Dutch people. The Nazis in Germany had been shown pictures and caricatures in newspapers and magazines of Jews with long hooked noses, black curly hair, and fat stomachs. When the Nazis came in Holland there were quite a few Jews that were like the Dutch: blond hair and blue eyes.

Bram had red hair and blue eyes, our children and I had blond or red hair and blue eyes. We blended in with the Dutch population. To the Germans we looked like Aryans. But for the Dutch people, who were used to our northern looks, there might have been other characteristics that, maybe, made them more aware of the Jews around. But it was always a dangerous risk to confront strangers, because we could not rely on looks or anything else.

Bram never showed himself. He was always alone upstairs in our room. I had to play the role of the Rotterdam woman with her husband in Germany. I had to be believable and that gave problems too. One day, a lady that lived close by invited me for tea. There was no sensible explanation to refuse, so I had to accept. And after a while I felt obliged to ask her back.

She came upstairs in our room. Bram was hiding in the closet, and for all the time that that woman was sitting there, comfortable, sipping her tea, Bram was standing there, straight, right behind the closetdoor, not able to move, cough, or even breathe too loud. Terrible. It seemed hours before she felt like leaving.

The only consolation it gave was that I was believable and accepted as a gentile Dutch lady.

34

Secret Police

Because so many houses had been bombed and the Germans that needed places to stay, there was an acute shortage of housing in Holland.

Then the Germans ordered everybody to share their homes. "Officially," Mrs. Straub lived alone in her big house with just her household staff.

After a while, an elderly gentleman came to live in that house. He was a military looking man in civilian clothes, a retired captain of the Dutch army, who wrote war statistics. He talked with nobody, and nobody knew anything more about him.

Soon after that, a family—man, wife and two children—bombed out of Arnhem, came to live there too. Mrs. Straub disliked the intrusion of this noisy family that were forced upon her by the Germans and occupied part of her house. So, for a while, all these people went their own way in the old house, and used the kitchen in turn, and tried to avoid problems. Because everybody that lived in that house felt removed from their regular lives, there was tension.

And the occupation we felt closely, and the war that was going on just around it, made it worse.

Bram and I had trained ourselves to be alert at all times. Even, or especially, when we went to bed. Also, when we undressed, we put our clothes on the chair in a certain order, and memorized it. If, suddenly, in the night, a raid or any other danger would arise, we could dress ourselves in the dark and try to hide out or escape. Bram was alert to all possibilities all those years.

Somehow we never had a relaxed, deep sleep. Even in our sleep, our senses seem to be alert. We got such a need for sleep that whenever we thought about the end of the war, it would be about the luxury that we finally might be able to close our eyes and really sleep. Not to be half-awake, listening for noises that might mean danger. Not to fear anymore that we might be raided at night and pulled away to an unknown fate. But to know that we would wake up the next morning in the same bed.

Then, one night, we heard noises around the house and in the house. We were worrying through the night, and in the morning we heard the dangerous truth. The Gestapo had during the night requisitioned and occupied the downstairs floor completely, to set up headquarters there.

Mrs. Underhill had prevented them from going upstairs by telling them that the upstairs rooms were not as good.

So here we were, like being in a lion's den, living with the Gestapo in the same house.

The Gestapo were the worst kind of Nazis. They were fanatic persecutors.

Right away, the tension in the house rose to a point of explosion.

They ordered Pleuntje to cook and fry for them. The woman from Arnhem did the washing for them, and me, they just hindered me. But every word was an interrogation.

Where is your husband? What country? What city? How long have you been here? Do you get letters from your husband? Does he send you money? And on and on.

Bram, always alert to danger, had foreseen this and had trained me right away to give the right answers. I owe much to Bram's foresight, his intelligence, and him teaching me. But I was always afraid that the Nazis could look through me and that I would make a fatal mistake.

Also, they started to harass the other women in the house. One of the soldiers told Mrs. Underhill he would come upstairs some evening to her room. She warned everybody upstairs to lock or block the doors. Nobody was sure what he would do or would discover.

It happened one day that an officer stood in my way on the stairs. I could not walk down. He asked me to go with him for a walk.

I answered him that I was married and that people would talk about me if I was going out with him. I said it all in an apologizing way. But he insisted, and he became not only difficult, but also sort of threatening.

I was afraid to make him angry. I did not know what to say anymore, and I was trapped.

My fear was so strong that I wanted to run back upstairs. But I realized that would have betrayed us all.

There I was. Being Jewish and hiding out with my family, and face-to-face with an angry Gestapo. I was afraid that he could look right through me and know. I could not handle this.

Suddenly that Dutch captain, who wrote the war statistics, came up to the stairs, excused himself in an arrogant, high-ranking military sort of way, pushed the Nazi aside while he walked upstairs, and gave me the chance to go on. The Nazi was bluffed. That captain saved me from unknown difficulties. And we never had exchanged a word as long as we were in that house.

I like to thank him now.

Figure 1. Judic with brother Max and mother Clara.

Figure 2. Judic with her parents, Clara and Isaac, 1932.

Figure 3. Brother Max, mother Clara, and Judic.

Figure 4. Judic's parents, Isaac de Vries and Clara Visser.

Figure 5. Right to left: Judic, her mother Clara, brother Max, father Isaac, and staff in one of the family's fabric stores, Utrecht.

Figure 6. Max in front of his fabric store, Zeist.

Figure 7. Judic and Max with their mother Clara, Utrecht.

Figure 8. Judic and Max with their father Isaac, Utrecht.

Secret Police | 131

Figure 9. Judic at the beach.

Figure 10. Judic as bridesmaid to cousin Chelly Visser.

Figure 11. Judic de Vries.

Figure 12. Abraham (Bram) Wijnberg.

Figure 13. Bram's mother, Alida Nathans-Wijnberg.

Figure 14. Bram's father, Samuel Asser Wijnberg, 1931.

Figure 15. Left to right: Bram (twenty) with sister Selma (fourteen), and brothers Marthijn (seventeen, standing) and Maurits Wijnberg (nineteen), March 1937.

Figure 16. Selma and Bram dancing.

Figure 17. Bram (seated holding gun, third from left) in army.

Figure 18. Max de Vries (standing) in army.

Figure 19. Wedding portrait of Judic and Bram, 8 May 1940. Selma Wijnberg seated by Judic and cousin Helena de Vries by Bram.

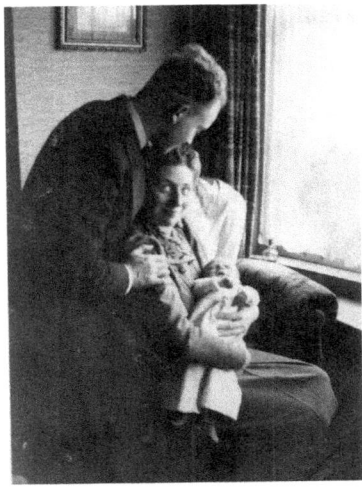

Figure 20. Judic, Bram, and infant Leo.

Figure 21. Alida Nathans-Wijnberg holding grandson Leo.

Figure 22. Leo with Obbe and Marie Faber.

Figure 23. Hotel Wijnberg with name painted on side wall.

Figure 24. Market opposite Hotel Wijnberg.

Figure 25. Judic holding Claire, Bram holding Alice; Jack (L), and Leo (R) in front, 1946.

Figure 26. Alice (L) and Claire (R) with goat in front of Hotel Wijnberg.

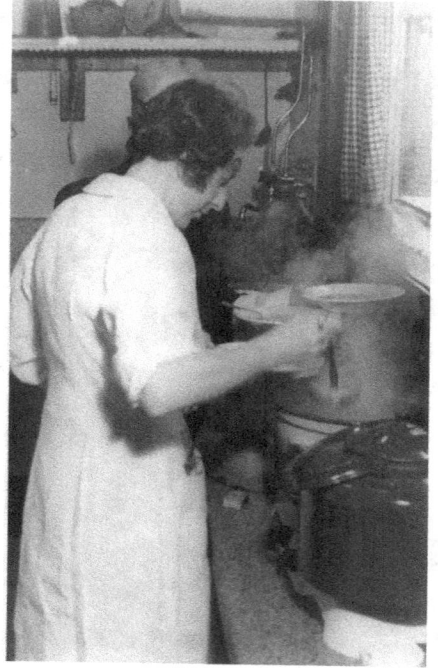

Figure 27. Judic in the kitchen of Hotel Wijnberg.

Figure 28. Hotel Wijnberg main floor restaurant.

Figure 29. Bram by copper coffee urns in Hotel Wijnberg.

Figure 30. Back row, from right to left: Selma, Chaim, Judic, and Bram, with friends.

Figure 31. Left to right: Jack, Claire, Judic, Leo, Alice, and Bram.

Secret Police | 143

Figure 32. Bram and Judic at Dam Square, Amsterdam.

Figure 33. Hotel Wijnberg with living room addition.

Figure 34. Inside new living room.

Figure 35. Leo (L) and Jack (R) with trailer on family trip, summer 1953.

Figure 36. Wijnberg family with Obbe and Marie Faber (wearing hats) and Beier (hotel headwaiter) before boarding the *Veendam* in Rotterdam, 1953.

Figure 37. Family on board the *Veendam* en route to North America, 1953.

Figure 38. Arrival of truck with belongings from Holland to College Street, Toronto. Left to right: Judic, Bram, and Leo.

Secret Police | 147

Figure 39. The house on Charleswood Drive, Toronto, 1954.

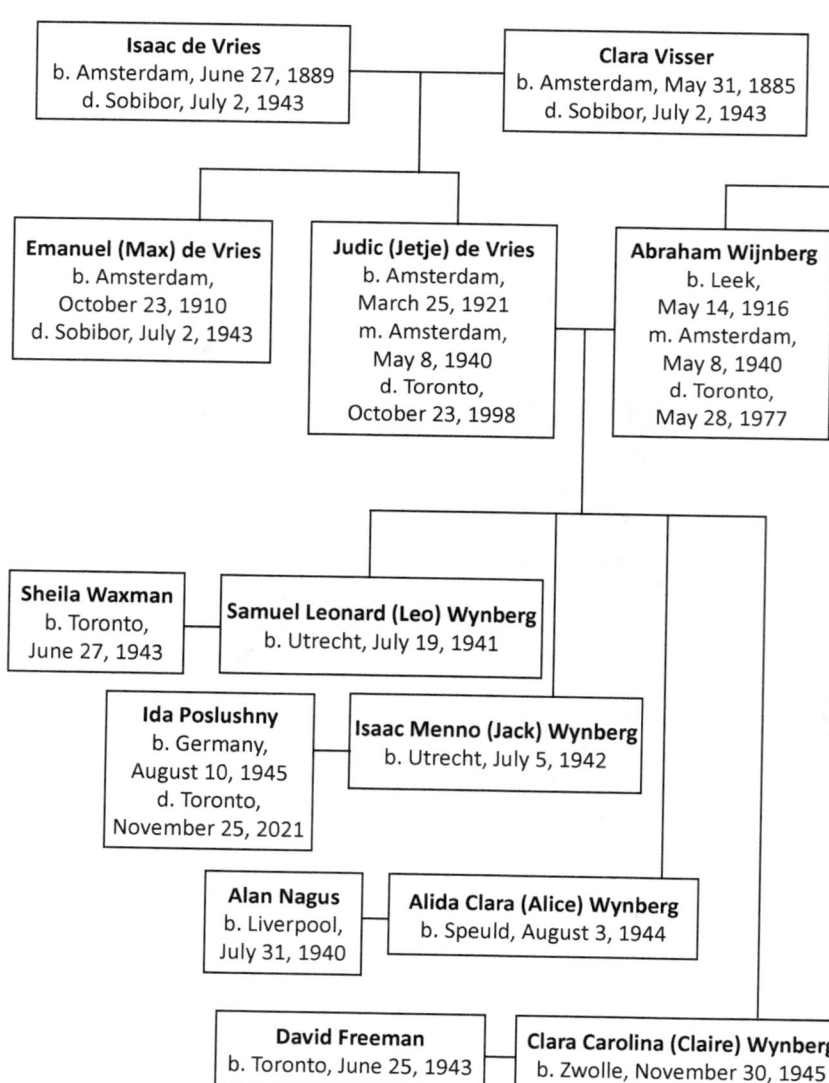

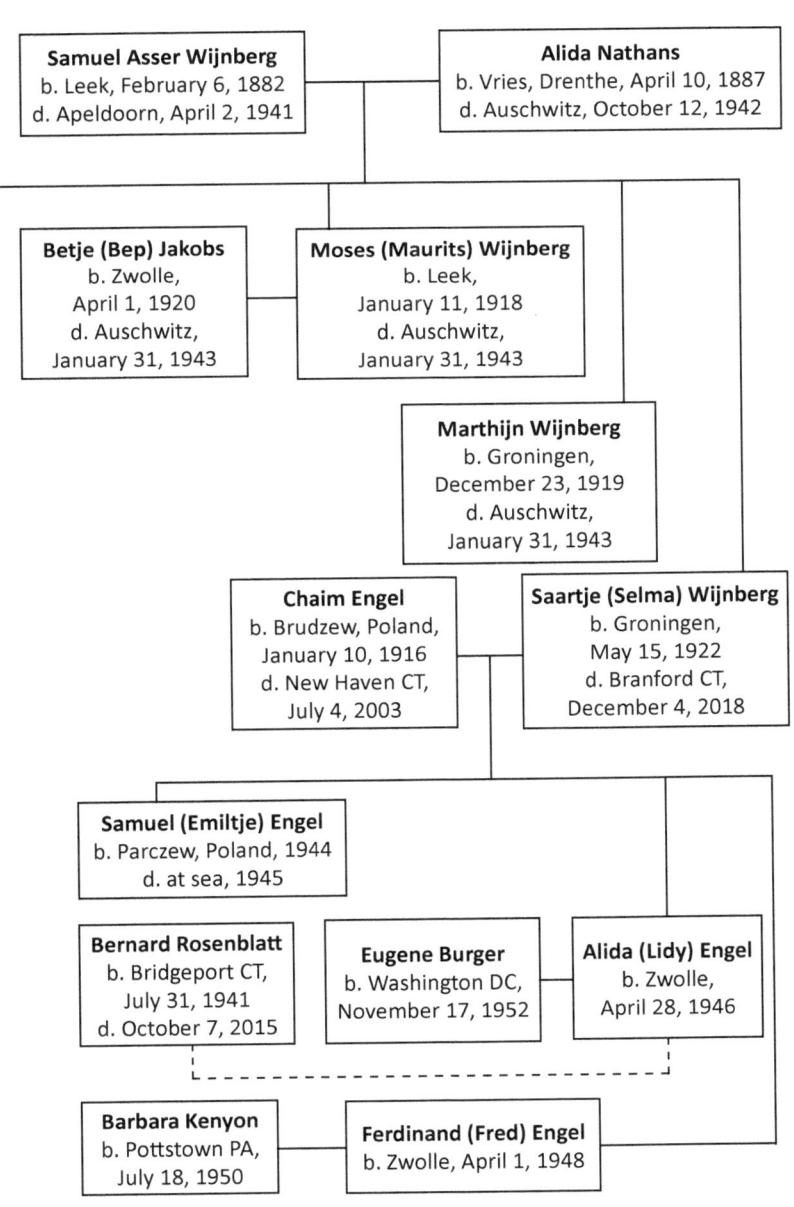

35

The Park-keeper

As always in times like that, some people became scared of the authorities and offensive to people in a difficult position. Or they just wanted to show the authorities how cooperative they were. In short, somebody had been talking around that the woman with the baby was a Jewess. The source of the talk seemed to be the park-keeper. We were in danger of being exposed. It had to be stopped before it was too late.

Bram suggested that he would talk to the man. It was dangerous because of the possibility that the park-keeper would discover that Bram was a Jew and my husband. But somebody had to talk to the traitor, and Bram had a plan. He took it up with Mrs. Underhill and she discussed with Mrs. Straub. Then Mrs. Straub sent a message to the park-keeper and ordered him to appear.

He came. A tall, sly man.

In the room were Mrs. Straub, Mrs. Underhill, and a man the park-keeper had never seen before. That strange man looked serious and stern. Mrs. Underhill introduced Bram as head of an underground organization.

Bram asked Mrs. Straub: "Mrs. Straub, is this your park-keeper, Jan?"

Mrs. Straub nodded.

And then Bram turned to the man: "Jan, the underground organization got to know that you talk about a Jewess here in the house. You understand that with such talk you endanger the members of this household, which we cannot and will not tolerate. You better behave in another fashion, because if anything happens to that woman, in any form, the underground will have to do away with you. You understand?"

The park-keeper looked at the face of his Lady, who looked superior, and Mrs. Underhill, who looked angry, and the strange man, who looked dangerous! He whispered, "Yes, sir."

When Bram dismissed him with "You can go now," he almost crawled, backing out of the door.

The betraying park-keeper had been an instant and serious danger. That Bram had thought of such a bold solution still impresses me. If he had made a wrong move or had said a wrong word, the park-keeper could have become suspicious and his life would have been in danger. Also me, his wife, and his baby. And others maybe. Also, they had put their confidence in Bram, and Bram showed intelligence and courage.

Writing about it now and thinking back, I wonder about Bram and me. We both came from good, middle-class families and lived a normal life. A young man and a young woman with hopes for a life together and a family. Instead, for many years, we became overwhelmed by dangerous and life-threatening situations. We never had a restful time together. How come we could handle it the way we did? We carried on. We had to. Our parents and Max would have wanted it. We had children. Maybe we wanted to live and we behaved in a style that we thought natural and might be expected from us.

Because I had to be in the kitchen for warming up Alida's milk-bottle, I could not help mingling with the Nazis. I could not avoid it. We had two young children who needed us and we were responsible for.

I never started any talk with them.

But one day a Nazi walked up to me and said he thought I could speak English. I told him I was not good but knew some words. He asked me to teach him some English. He would like to learn.

So it happened that I, a young Jewish woman, with her family hiding out from the Nazis, gave one of them English lessons. A strange and dangerous situation. And although I could speak German, I tried not to be good in either language. That might have been out of character. Again, how come I handled it that way? Everything we did and every word we spoke had to be thought out. Never allowed to make a mistake. Having presence of mind. Bram and me, just two young people. Being in danger and always having to react right. Maybe God directed us this way. Maybe.

So many times Bram had to act and take risks, taking our sons from the Nazi-guarded building, and handling the park-keeper. And Max was in the resistance. My parents and Max gave their lives to make our leaving safer.

Don't let anybody say that the Dutch Jews went like sheep. If there was no other chance possible, they went with dignity. Who are others to criticize?

There was Dr. Perel, who came to me after curfew. There was Dr. Susskind, a Jew who tried to save babies from the transports. Courage is not only in killing the enemy. It is also in protecting a human being—man, woman, or child—whose life is threatened by an enemy. I loved and respected my parents and brother and Bram for their courage and love.

We did not feel brave or smart. We were so afraid. But still there was courage. It is sad that criticism often comes from Jews. Maybe afraid for (of) their own image. Maybe self-hate. Or just lack of understanding.

***

Although it was not a real castle, the old house had a special atmosphere that put a certain behaviour on the people that lived in it. There were long halls and high ceilings and intriguing antiques. In one of the halls was a big antique blanket chest, and somewhere else stood a huge antique grandfather clock.

Somebody, probably Pleuntje or Mrs. Underhill, had told me that there were a lot of books upstairs in the attic and I could read them if I wanted. So one day, I walked upstairs to the attic. When I looked around there, I was impressed.

It was quite a big library and there were also all kinds of other interesting things to look at.

Happy about that, I opened a book. It was about spiritism. I put it back and opened another one. Again about spiritism. I walked to the other side of the attic to look for other books. But what I opened were all about spiritism and about the unknown life of the trees and plants around us. They were books of Mrs. Straub's personal interest.

I became very uncomfortable, which was not surprising. This old house had high ceilings and slightly curved stairs. Because of the blackout, the house was not lighted, and at night we walked around with a candle which created shadows. To be alone in the attic surrounded by books about spiritism made me feel uncomfortable, and in my hurry to leave I stumbled downstairs. And it had been daylight.

In the evening and at night the Germans kept a strict check on the house for a total blackout. They had set up headquarters in the house, and there were always English planes flying over. That bothered them.

One night, a Nazi came upstairs and just walked into our room to tell us that our curtains were not closed enough for the blackout.

There we were, Mrs. Straub, Mrs. Underhill, Bram, and I, playing bridge by candlelight. Bram's presence could not be explained and the shock made us quiet.

The Nazi started to holler, but as we were so quiet he apologized for coming in like that. But he repeated that we had to keep a strict blackout and have our curtains better closed. Then the Nazi left us, without questioning Bram. Thank God.

36

A Hiding Place

It seemed for a short while that we had no immediate problem.

But then Hermann, the boyfriend of Pleuntje, became troublesome. He was originally German and he wanted us out of Pleuntje's life.

One day, he came up to Bram and said it was too dangerous for everybody and that we should leave. He said it was easy for the Nazis to find us there and expose us.

Bram denied that.

Then Hermann gave him an ultimatum.

We should hide out and he would look for us, and if he could find us we had to leave. Or else? If he could not find us, he said he would let us be. He was threatening us and we did not trust him.

It was terrible.

Bram discussed what to do with Mrs. Underhill, and she talked with Mrs. Straub about it. And then, that very old lady, Mrs. Straub, came out in her very old age as a woman with a very strong mind.

She could not talk very good anymore, but she took Bram up to a little room next to ours. There was only a desk and a chair in that little room, and on the striped wallpaper did hang some paintings. That was all.

Nothing could hide there!

Then the old lady showed that she knew the secrets of the old house.

There was a painting hanging high on the wall. She made clear to Bram that he had to move it a little bit aside.

And there it was! An entrance to a hiding place connecting our room with this room! Right under the ceiling in the wall. Camouflaged by the striped wallpaper and covered by the painting!

That had always been there and only the old lady knew.

Hermann looked everywhere in the house for us. He did not find us.

Thanks to a very old Dutch lady, who could not talk very well anymore but had a strong mind and a gentle character.

In resisting the Nazis, she did her share.

37

A Dangerous Man

The war and occupation had been going on for about four years now. Bram and I, being Jews, were daily under stress because, as Jews under the Nazi rule, our lives could be endangered by anybody who had an antisemitic or pro-Nazi attitude.

Our only defense was to recognize certain ways in their behaviour or talking that could give us a hint. We were alert. Very alert. Any small detail, ignored by everybody else, could give us a warning. We must not be discovered.

Once, while I was warming Lida's bottle in the kitchen, I heard one of those Green Police talk about the good life he had in Germany. He had lived in a big house, owned beautiful furniture, and had good paintings on the walls. He had lived a rich life there. But now it was war, and he was in the army.

I was right away alarmed. This man was dangerous! Without anybody realising it, he had conveyed that message to me, because we were always and always observing for telltale signs.

And while he went on telling that he later moved to a bigger house, and everybody listened to him and envied him, I began to tremble. To me the story was different and clear. This was a common man, this *polizei* member, in the army.

If he had lived rich, in different houses, it could only have been if he had been a traitor to Jewish families and had lived in their houses, looting their furniture and other belongings.

And while he went on talking, and everybody was listening and smiling, I realised that he was deeply involved in the persecution of Jews, had profited from it, and liked it.

I tried to be calm and inconspicuous, and walked away with the bottle to go upstairs and tell Bram. I would have liked to be invisible, but I had to act normal. At this time we could not change anything.

And we carried on, being still more alert. Nothing else we could do.

38

Radio Orange

The war went on, but it was hard to find out where the armies were. There was only the allowed and unreliable news from the censored Dutch newspapers that told us about all the victories of the Germans. Or that they had retreated "according to plans." Which the Dutch translated as the Germans were on the run. And there were, of course, all kind of rumours.

The English had started a radio station that was directed to Holland.

And they broadcasted news from the English army reports. They also reported about the fighting on the fronts and the locations. They gave reports about the movements of the Allied armies and the air force. If the English air force had flown deep into Germany and had hit their targets—a factory, a bridge, or dam—it was important news.

But maybe more important was that they sent messages to the Dutch resistance. The messages to the resistance were in code. And the locations of the fighters and saboteurs were always given as "somewhere in the Netherlands." Never any indication that might betray the hideouts of the resistance.

The ones that the message was meant for knew the code. A message that Joanna had visited Henk could mean that a certain bridge had been blown up. Or an Allied parachutist had landed "somewhere in the Netherlands."

The name of the radio station was Radio Orange.

Of course, the Germans made it a crime to listen to Radio Orange, and if somebody was betrayed and caught, it meant imprisonment, or worse!

But people wanted to know and some had a radio and listened. Then they did tell the news to people they trusted.

Sometimes, when it was dark outside, some people came to the Castle and went to the kitchen to tell and discuss the news. It was dark inside too because for blackout the curtains were closed and only one candle was lighted.

There was a strange atmosphere in that darkened kitchen. We did not really know each other, but we had to trust each other not to be a traitor. We could not see each other's faces with the one candle flickering and making shadows. But somehow, by being together, knowing that we were all at risk for our lives, we still might have felt some strength that being alone maybe not always gives. But Bram still had to be invisible. He remained in the back of the darkest shadow.

It was a mixed gathering in that darkened kitchen. Some anti-Nazi Dutchmen, Bram and me (two Jews hiding out), some resistance fighters, and Mrs. Underhill.

If a Nazi would have walked in, there was no explanation possible for all of us being there.

And personal identification cards would mostly be counterfeit.

There was tension.

When afterwards Bram and I went upstairs to our room again, Bram discussed the news, and it was remarkable how well he could predict what to expect from the army movements and the political behaviour of the different governments.

But that, for us, our only chance on living was to remain in hiding.

For how much longer?

39

Hunger Winter—1944

The war went on. The years passed and the seasons changed.

Another summer had gone, there was a short fall, and we started to feel the cold of the winter. When Mrs. Straub and I were on the daily walk through her park, she noticed that the trees in her park were disappearing.

The people around there came at night, cut the trees, and took them home for heating their stoves and houses.

Food became scarce. The German army in Holland had to be fed by the Dutch. And that is where the cows went for milk and meat. And that was where the eggs went and the bread and the sugar. And everything else.

Hollanders themselves became hungry.

Especially in the big cities.

And people from the big cities went to the country, to the farmers, and tried to exchange things for food. Money was not important.

So they came with their tablecloths and weddingrings and cutlery, or whatever was possible. They went to the farmers trying to trade it in for flour, potatoes, or bacon.

The farms around the cities were soon empty. Then the winter weather turned extremely cold. And in this bitter cold, streams of hungry people walked days and nights, from farm to farm, from village to village. They walked to far away farms in the hope of buying some food.

They all had to walk because the Germans had "requisitioned" just about everything that had wheels.

"Requisitioning" or "confiscating" were just official-sounding words for looting and stealing by the German soldiers. They also seized the food.

Then the Dutch people—men, women, some very young ones—had to keep walking because at their homes their hungry dependents waited for their return...

In the Castle we felt a shortage too. We ate watery porridge and drank substitute coffee without sugar.

Mrs. Underhill tried to keep everybody eating. Bram, of course, paid for our share, but there was not much available.

Then Mrs. Underhill, without telling Mrs. Straub, started some trading on her own. She told the farmers around the Castle that they could cut some trees if they provided food. This way, Mrs. Underhill obtained some sugarbeets.

And then Bram and I were grating down sugarbeets day after day, for days in a row. They were stonehard. The pulp was boiled and it became a sugary syrup that we used as sweetener.

It was hard work and everything became sticky. Even the walls.

Holland, winter 1944. It was cold. There was occupation and war. There were cold and hungry people walking through the country in search for food to take home to their families. Sometimes their food was taken by the Nazis. Some of those Dutch people died on the road from cold and exhaustion.

That was Holland, the *hongerwinter* (Hunger Winter) of 1944.

Time seemed to slow down somehow.

At night, we heard the English bomberplanes go over to their targets in Germany. Hundreds and hundreds were high in the sky. They made a heavy droning sound, which reassured us that something was being done against a mutual enemy. But the Nazis had been long preparing for a destructive war.

Suddenly, they came out with a secret new weapon. The V-1. It was a rocket that could be directed to a faraway target in England, and when coming down on it was very destructive.

The first ones we heard sounded frightening. It was as if a big, heavy, iron train on rails was riding right on the roof of your home. You automatically ducked down for cover. And even after finding out what it was, the fear remained, because many of those V-1s were faulty and sometimes made a turn and could fall down and explode anywhere in Holland. Or sometimes they just failed in midair and could come down and explode on your home.

Soon after that, an improved rocket came out, which was called the V-2. And then the Germans used the Christmas season to double their destruction in England.

Some more time went by. But Jews, at all times during the war, were being prosecuted by the Nazis or betrayed by collaborators. There was forever the fear to be discovered and exposed. We were surrounded by Gestapo. Every move we made, or every word I said, had to be thought out.

Then the tension that was in the house all that time finally exploded. The woman from Arnhem, on insistence from her husband, refused to wash for the Nazi officers. And then one of them made a clear threat that he would get her for that. And he added: "Also everybody else in this house!"

That same day, the complete family from Arnhem had left the house. Nobody knew where they could have gone so fast. They had left, and left the rest of us to face the consequences.

Bram decided we had to leave too, as fast as possible. But how? And where? The three of us. Bram wanted to talk to farmer de Liever and ask him to find another place for us.

We knew he belonged to the underground. We went there at dusk, Bram and I together. I had a milk pitcher in my hand to make it look like a regular trip for food. Bram talked with the farmer about our position. De Liever suggested that I should stay a little longer in the Castle, but that Bram would become another farmhand. This way we could try to avoid suspicion. After that was agreed upon, Bram and I had to go back.

In the meantime, it had become dark, and we were just walking a little footpath through some bushes back to the Castle. Suddenly, from the dark, a voice came loud: "*Werda!*"—which is German and means "Who is it?" but was being used to stop you. And again, "*Werda!*" We saw the glinting of a gun. Then, out of the dark, somebody else started to talk and answer the Nazi. Bram whispered to me: "Cover your face and run!" And we did. The Nazi had the other man and decided that was easier prey than going after us.

Later on, I asked Bram why I had to cover my face with my coat. He told me that our faces were light against the dark evening and that it should be camouflaged so that the Nazi could not see us so easy. Bram had been a soldier and knew those things. Bram again had been alert and acted intelligent. Or was it one of those strange coincidences that we had experienced before? There was that man in the dark bushes who had occupied the Nazi. God, Bram, fate, and so many other coincidences that had happened in our lives.

There is no answer...

40

Canadian Soldiers

The war seemed to come closer. We heard more shooting and bombing. It became louder. We tried to find out what was happening. But nobody knew, or nobody talked.

It was about that time we knew I was pregnant again. Mrs. van Binsbergen came to visit us once and asked if we were all right. She was really concerned. We told her that if our next baby was a girl, she would also be named after her—Carolina.

The Gestapo that lived in the Castle started to act different. Sometimes they went out in the middle of the night. We heard rumours about their nightly killing sprees of saboteurs and underground fighters.

Or just killings.

And then they were gone!

Suddenly, in the middle of the night, like the way they had come. We found later some Nazi uniforms buried in the parkgrounds! The next morning, they were replaced by Hitlerjugend (Hitler Youth) fighters. Those Hitlerjugend were young, wild, and arrogant. And unpredictable.

One morning, we found out that some bridges in the neighbourhood had been blown up.

There was a strange atmosphere of waiting for what would happen next. For a few days that lasted. Waiting and contradictory movements from the Hitlerjugend, who went out to see if they could fight somewhere. And then that stopped too, and they disappeared also in the night.

Rumours went around that Canadian soldiers were nearing Zwolle, and that there were some skirmishes.

Then, on a beautiful morning in May, we woke up to a changed atmosphere.

The Dutch had seen for the first time Canadian soldiers on the ground! Altogether only three soldiers. We did not dare to believe it.

But Bram said: "We are going outside! Come on, Jet, let us go and walk outside together! It is over."

I was still afraid to give up our cover. But Bram and I went outdoors, arm in arm, and I proudly shouted: "This is my husband! We are free now!"

And I introduced him to all those surprised people that only had seen me for more than a year. We walked there outdoors and talked to everybody. It was really true. The Canadians had told Bram that there were Canadian troops in Zwolle and that more would come. Bram right away spoke English with them. They liked that because they could not speak Dutch.

Wapenveld, Holland.

Yes, it was a nice morning in May 1945.

41

Suddenly Free

Later in the day, Bram and I walked together outside, in the sun, quietly. It was such a deep experience. Outside under the trees and the sun.

And walking, just the two of us, on a country road, we suddenly stood in front of a Nazi soldier, who was standing guard there. I could still feel the fear for his past authority. And my mind told me to run, because how could we already be sure that his power was really gone? The power to take us prisoner for just being Jews. The fear we have had all those years for this uniform was not completely gone yet. Somebody or something was out of place.

And we assured ourselves that it was the German soldier who did not belong there.

Finally, that became clear. We took a deep breath and walked on. Trying to enjoy and feel free.

The next day, Bram wanted to cross the IJssel River and go to Zwolle. I was still afraid and had to stay with Lida. The bridges around were blown up or might be undermined with explosives.

So Bram went to Zwolle with somebody in a rowboat to cross the IJssel. I waited all day, and later in the evening he came back. Then Bram started to talk about the Canadian army he had seen in Zwolle, and saying hello and greeting and thanking them. And about the funny old-fashioned little cars they had which they called Jeeps.

How he had been walking in the streets and not getting enough of it. He had gone to his hotel and greeted the neighbours. He went on and on.

He crossed the IJssel again, and came back to tell me: "We are free!"

Suddenly Bram broke down. Completely. He said he felt sick and was going to die.

He went to bed. Maybe he cried. And maybe he was sick. But it must have been a shock to realize now, when it was over, how close we often had been to death. The responsibilities he had taken and carried, and the risks he had to take. The decisions he had made, life and death decisions. The way we had lived, especially Bram. Being in one room. Sleeping stretched out under a floor. Standing immovable in a closet. Always in danger. For many, many years.

Freedom was still unbelievable and too new to absorb. He wanted to give up and die. Right then.

And I told him: "It is all over now. Now you are going to live. We are free."

He was still shocked for a while, some days. And he did not seem anxious to come out of it. But he did. And again, he took up the load of responsibilities and decision-making. "We are leaving," he said. "We are going to Zwolle and to our hotel, to our home, to live."

So Bram and I and Lida went to our home in Zwolle:
<u>HOTEL WIJNBERG</u>

42

Coming Home

We did go to Zwolle. And we went to the Veemarkt, Bram, Lida, and I saw there the hotel in front of us. Bram walked steady up to it, but I had a hesitant feeling as if I still was a fugitive, an underdiver, and that we really did not have the right to walk into our own home.

But we went in.

It was a chaotic mess! Later on, we heard that German troops had lived there, and before leaving it, ruined and dirtied as much as they could. And after that they wanted to set the hotel on fire. That was prevented by some Dutch men.

We walked through the house and it was a disgusting sight everywhere. In the cellar the Germans had kept the coal for the furnace and also potatoes for the kitchen.

Before leaving they had mixed them completely up and made both impossible to be used.

The entrance to the winecellar was blocked with garbage. We just had to throw everything out. Piles and piles of dirt and junk.

Bram went out to look for cleaning help and came back with an old woman that used to work for his mother. Also came back the old gardener, Versteeg, who started to put the big garden in order, and with his scythe did cut the grass. When I looked at him doing that, it gave me a sense of order and peace.

Then Bram went to Utrecht and brought Jack home, and we all went to Friesland for a few days, to rest with Obbe and Marie on their farm and give the children the chance to be together after all that time.

It had been hard for the van Brummelens, who saw Jack as their son, to let him go.

Also for Obbe and Marie, who had adopted Leo. They wanted to give him comfort and bring him up in their Christian religion, and he would later inherit the farm. They even offered to keep Jack also.

But Bram explained that we wanted to have our young sons at home with us, with their family, and the surroundings that belonged to them.

Finally, we had our family, Leo, Jack and Alida, together, and we went back to our hotel in Zwolle. Our home.

Now, back with our family in the hotel, we had to make it clean and liveable again.

It took us weeks and weeks, and pails and pails of water and soap, and scrubbing and working and washing, and still throwing dirt out, before we got it fairly clean. But the hotel was empty. There was nothing to start business with.

Bram had to become a detective and inquired around what had happened with the furniture, dishes, silver cutlery, carpets, linens, in short everything. He found out that his mother and brothers, before they had been taken, had placed part of the equipment with some customers and friends, for safekeeping. And so Bram followed that lead and came up with quite a bit of the original contents. But not enough.

So again, he went out and bought and gathered whatever we needed. Somehow Bram got the idea to search the backyard. There he found some pewter pitchers that his brothers had buried there. They used to be very nice, but now the chemistry in the ground had ruined them.

The hotel business started to take shape. Bram contacted and hired his old waiters and also hired cleaning women and a live-in maid. Finally, he approached his old customers, renewed the friendship with them, and told them the opening date. And that all the first drinks for his customers, and whoever they might want to bring in, were on the house.

We opened the next Friday cattlemarket and there was a big wellwishing crowd! And so Hotel Wijnberg regained its place.

The name "Hotel Wijnberg" was brought back where it belonged, painted on top of the side wall, for everybody to see.

Bram carried on his family name and the family business. It was right.

It was about that time, on a nice day, Bram looked up, shocked, and ran outside. There was Selma, shouting loud: "Bram, Bram!" They both ran and fell in each other's arms, and they cried. Selma introduced Chaim, her Polish husband. After escaping from camp Sobibor, they had been hiding out with a Polish farmer.

Then Selma got her share of the hotel and Chaim started to work in it. Gradually, we came to the end of our first summerseason back home. At the beginning of the fall, Bram started to prepare for the busy winter season of the hotel. He sent out letters and cards to all kinds of clubs saying that in the coming winterseason he would have a ballroom available for parties and also would give dancing instruction.

And when the first lessons started, and Bram was counting the rhythm of the dance steps to the music—slow, slow, quick-quick, slow—I got my labourpains and was rushed to the hospital.

Our fourth baby, a girl, was born. Our first baby born in freedom.

But thank God, we had survived. Bram and I and our four children were together and home. The baby, Claire, was named after my mother, Clara, and a woman that helped to save our lives, Carolina.

Bram, who was a certified teacher of ballroom dancing, had soon his evenings filled with clubs to teach the latest steps and the new dances that came out. He was a good teacher, and in a national dance school competition, one of Bram's clubs won a medal.

He was quite popular.

At the first anniversary celebration of Holland's freedom, Bram was requested to lead a ball outdoors, in the city square. There was a big band, and Bram was leading a polonaise through the streets of Zwolle, for thousands and thousands of people.

He was in his glory!

Time went by with hard work. Jack and Leo went to school, and a year later Alida also. Claire was still too young.

When the other kids were in school, Claire felt lonely. Bram went to a teacher about accepting her, but it was against the school rules, and maybe against the law, for children to enter school before they were six years old. Claire would be six in November and the school had started in September. She would almost lose a year. What could be done was to teach her at home grade one subjects, and if she was at par with other children at the time, then she could start school in grade two. And so I taught Claire grade one with the help of a teacher, and in the following September she started school in the second grade.

When at home, the kids were looked after by Aartje, a live-in farmers daughter.

We had a good time. We went for trips and camping in summer and the kids sleighing and skiing in winter.

At school they did very well. And at home they ran out on Aartje all around the cattlemarket when it was bedtime. Claire and Alida went to ballet classes and had a goat for a pet. Leo and Jack learned judo, and all four were supposed to learn to play the piano.

One day, Chaim and Selma said they wanted to get their share of the hotel paid out to them because they were going to be partners in a textile store.

So that left only our family behind in the hotel.

We were survivors.

And so were other Jews. Selma had even survived the concentrationcamp Sobibor. She told us that in camp, while sorting out clothes from prisoners, she had found family pictures from our wedding. Pa, Mom, and Max had carried those pictures with them.

And after she had told us that, I started to look out of the window, in the direction from where Selma had come back. I did not believe that my parents would have survived, but I gave myself the hope, that maybe Max, a young man, could... maybe...

For a long time, I was always looking, and wishing, maybe... hoping, without hope.

Nobody came to me...

And instead came the thoughts about how they must have ended their lives in terror. The transport by wagons, without food or drink, nor even a place to sit down.

The long dark ride, going away from home, without knowledge about their destination.

And at arrival somewhere far away, the separation from each other, and the final realisation of their deaths.

Bram and I never talked about it. But I just know that we both tried to identify with our family as victims. We could not.

Maybe we are not allowed to intrude in a man's private suffering. Bram might have had the same thoughts, but we never discussed it. These thoughts you suffer alone. Even Bram and I. And maybe especially Bram and I. I don't blame myself about having thought about that so much. But I blame myself that because of that I was losing touch of my responsibilities within the realities of the present.

We had to carry on and bring up our children with the best values we knew of. And in doing so give them a link with their grandparents and uncles, who would have loved them so much if they had been allowed to live. We had to be the link that connects them, our children, with our roots.

43

So Many Lost

Pa, Mom and Max, left concentrationcamp Westerbork at the end of June 1943. Selma found pictures of our wedding in camp Sobibor, so probably my family had been there and been killed after arrival.

Later on, there was an uprising in Sobibor. A short time after the uprising, Himmler ordered the destruction of this death camp. And then they planted grain and grass where barracks and death used to be. They tried to hide their crimes against thousands and thousands of Jews. They tried to hide the crime of killing my family.

Bram's father had died in the beginning of the occupation of Holland. Bram's mother, his brother Maurits and his wife Bep Jacobs, just married, and his talented younger brother Marthijn, we had no sure information what happened to them. Maybe Auschwitz.

Much later, when I told Bram not to be so much absorbed anymore in the past and the dead, he answered me: "They have the right to be remembered!"

We remembered our family. Every day. For many years. We thought of them how much they had meant to us. How we missed them around us. How we still needed them. As people, as family.

But our background faded away.

Or maybe we did not want to face the emptiness around us. Otherwise, I cannot explain that while we were free, and sometimes travelled, we never went back to Utrecht, to our old homes.

We never went back to the street where we had the store and lived.

We never went back to the home where my parents and Max had lived and from where I went to the hospital to have our sons. In Amsterdam, we never went back to the houses where our uncles and aunts had lived in. The houses of our family where we knew to be welcome.

Strange people lived in there now. Or maybe they were demolished. Destroyed and gone, like their residents. We did not go back and see what had happened. I realise that now, while thinking back. We never tried to find out what had happened to what once belonged to us. Bram might have inquired and accepted the answer that all was lost. We never went to our former neighbours for information. Maybe Bram did, and did not want to tell me. But I am not sure.

We knew our family was lost. We had no thought for anything else. We might have been afraid to face the actual emptiness.

We went on living. Not to look back.

The loss hardest to accept was that there were not even graves of them to visit.

Never to go back.

44

Displaced Persons

While we were getting settled after the war, there were still people in camps in Germany. They were people who in the war had lost their homes and family.

And their identity papers!

They had no place to go to and could not leave Germany without passports and other identity papers.

Those people without papers were termed "stateless" and became the "displaced persons." Even then, when the horror of the concentrationcamps was known, there was still no state anxious to give them asylum.

And so they stayed in camps...

One day, while working in the downstairs restaurant room, Bram was approached by a man who introduced himself as Janec. He wanted to talk to Bram privately. Bram took him aside to a table and they sat down.

Janec said he was Polish and was head of an escape organization.

What he and his helpers did was to get in contact with the displaced persons in the camps and helped and guided them at night to certain places where they could cross the border and enter Holland.

From there on they went on their way to Israel, the United States, Belgium, England, or wherever they had family or friends living and a chance to reach them.

There was an obstacle though about the right time of crossing. Dark nights.

And waiting for proceeding, they needed a place to stay.

We, being Jewish, and having a hotel, could be a big help if they could hide out with us, waiting for the right time. It had to be kept very quiet because it was an illegal act of crossing the border and immigration.

Bram right away said yes and opened the hotel for the transients. Without any charge for anything. We were not sure though whether Janec did not take advantage of that. But that was not our concern. We felt so good that finally we had a chance to give back some of the help we had received when we were hiding out.

Soon, in the middle of the night, there came the first group of displaced persons.

Our hearts became upset by looking at them. Not so long ago we had been in the same position.

There were old men with side curls, pregnant women, and men that were put down by their position in this life.

We made big tables with good and plenty of food, and encouraged them to eat. But they did not eat much, and some of them not at all. They were strictly kosher, and not knowing us, they took their own bread out of their pockets, broke it, and ate it. They just took coffee or tea.

They were all scared! We told them to sit in the garden, that this was Holland, that nothing serious could happen anymore.

But it did not help.

Bram told our friends, Lampel and Content and Hony, about it. They came with cigarettes and candies to treat them and trying to make them feel good.

The people were thanking everybody, but remained scared.

After a few days, sometime in the middle of the night, Janec came with new people, and took these away to bring them to the Belgium border.

The new group was of a different composition. Younger men and women, and a child of about three years old, and a baby.

We were wondering if the children did not make noise, or cried, by crossing such a long road at night. It could have betrayed them!

No, because Janec had instructed them to give the children some wine to drink so they would be drowsy and quiet.

There was one man in this group who ate and laughed the most. He annoyed the others. And then he said: "Of course I laugh and eat. Nothing can happen to me! I won't even die!"

Then he started to tell that he had been part of a group of Jews from a concentrationcamp who were to be executed by the Gestapo.

And they shot them in the neck.

By some sort of fate, the bullet had only hit the side of his neck and did not kill him.

And when the Gestapo threw the shot Jews into the river nearby, he was the last one to be thrown in. They skipped him because a row of army trucks came to pick up the Gestapo. So they left him, lying there in the middle of the road.

The trucks passed him without overrunning him. But his ankle was damaged. And after a while he became conscious and then crawled to his way for freedom!

Now he said: "Why shouldn't I laugh? What more can happen to me? You should laugh. Because we are all living and sitting here and have a good meal in front of us. What are you afraid of now?

What is wrong with eating?"

The other Jews were quiet.

There was also a young man in this group, who stayed a little longer because his uncle from Belgium would come to bring him home himself.

He liked me very much and asked if I would come to visit him in Belgium. I would be treated as family.

Lampel later took up his invitation, instead of me, and went there. The boy's uncle was a furrier in Belgium and an importer of Canadian skins.

45

Painful Words

I did a lot of cooking for the family. Of course I did the cooking for the restaurant on the Friday cattle market. Or when we were booked for luncheon meetings or simple dinner parties. Also when "our" soccerclub had won and came after the game with about hundred people to celebrate with drinks and coffee and sandwiches. For big gourmet style dinners Bram hired a chef.

Sometimes I assisted Bram when he was teaching ballroom dancing to his clubs and had not called in his assistant.

Yes, Bram was very well liked and business was good. But what had happened during the war and the Nazi occupation could not be ignored or forgotten. It had left its mark on the Gentiles as well as on the Jews.

There were moments that Bram lost his temper. It sometimes happened that a customer came up to Bram and, after saying hello, followed it up with the words: "So, you are still alive? The gaschambers did not get you?"

Or somebody else said: "You are back in business and making money again?" They tried to act as if it were common remarks. But we knew better. To our inner hearing, to our ability to size things up, and our war practice of noticing tell-tale signs, it was not good.

And Bram turned white. He wasted no answer but packed them up and threw them out. These were the traces of a poison that Hitler had left behind. Antisemitism. We knew that, and no light-making or denial would change that.

Oversensitive? We had reason to be! And knowing now the full truth about what had happened to our parents and brothers, Bram did not tolerate or ignore one insinuation or one wrong word.

There were people who proudly told us that they had known where Jews were hiding out but had not informed on them. But the people that really had fought in the resistance or had helped hiding out Jews did not talk about it. They, like we, felt resentment towards those negative people with their big talk now the danger was gone. That became sometimes a reason for bitterness for the underground who during the occupation had risked so much, but even after the war did not talk about it.

When Bram, after the war, tried to find the family Gerritse he encountered that. They did not live at the old address in Utrecht anymore. I think Bram traced them finally to Amsterdam. There he found, and came to talk with, Jaap Gerritse, the boy who was twelve years when he had brought Pa and Mom to his parents' house while praying all the way to God for safety. He had grown into a young man who wanted to become a professional and went to high school. Bram asked him why he was not in university yet. And then Jaap told Bram about his trouble at school, being the oldest in class because he had lost years during the war.

Bram was furious. He went to Jaap's high school and told his teachers there that Jaap had been part of the resistance and had risked his life while they were going to school, uninvolved. They should be proud to have him. When Bram noticed their surprised faces, he realized that Jaap had never talked about that. Which was really typical.

Before Bram left Jaap's school, all the teachers and the principal promised to help Jaap to catch up and help him to make up for lost time. It was going to be their belated contribution to a war effort. Jaap seemed more hopeful.

And then Bram said goodbye.

46

The "Safe-Keepers"

Then there were the "safe-keepers."

During the German occupation the Jews were not allowed to have any property. So they became an easy target for the Nazis and their followers, who in the name of confiscating for the government, robbed the Jews of anything they owned. Whether it was their homes and furniture, or their business, or their silver and jewellery. Even the money in their pockets had been confiscated for the government. It is easy to understand that most of it found its way to the pockets of the confiscators and their friends. The Jews really got plundered empty.

But the Jews needed to eat and had to buy food. And for that they needed some money for themselves.

Some Jews contacted some of their non-Jewish friends they trusted, and asked them to help them and save some money or valuables for them until they needed it or until the war was over. My father trusted his bookkeeper and gave him a fair amount of money and told him that he should give it to Bram and me if we were in trouble and needed it.

And Pa told us about the care he had taken for us.

It did not take long before Bram had to go to the bookkeeper (I remember his name) and ask him for some money of the amount that Pa had given him. But the bookkeeper flatly denied that he ever got a penny!

My father had trusted that man for many years while he had been in business.

But then it was war, and there was nothing Bram could do but leave fast, before he might even be handed over himself to the Nazis.

There were many Jews who had given in confidence their valuables to their non-Jewish friends, to keep it for the duration of the war.

After the war, the few Jews that came out alive, or sometimes just their children who had survived, asked for their property back. And in most cases it was handed back again.

But there were the greedy safe-keepers who were disappointed that "their" Jews had not died in the gaschambers, and were asking their property back. One of these cases was that of our friend Lampel.

They used to have a jewellery store. When they had to hide out, they accepted the offer of a neighbour who had a fishstore on the corner across the street. This neighbour would get Lampel's inventory of jewellery and save it for him.

After the war, when Lampel came back alive and asked if he could get back his stock so he could start business again, the answer was: "We got nothing from you!"

It was Thursday night when the Lampels came to our hotel and told us what had happened. They were quite upset.

We were sitting in a curtained off part of the downstairs restaurant. Having guests on Thursday night that do business on the Friday morning market, there was quite an audience that heard about that calculated setup. The worst was, it could not be proven because it had to be a secret maneuver at the time. So it would be Lampel's word against the neighbour fishman.

There seemed to be no solution. Police or court would have the same problem. Word of one against another one.

While we were all listening, there came an atmosphere of anger and solidarity in the room.

Was this still possible after all that had happened? The war was over. Had nothing changed after the war?

Our guests left the next day after the market and went to their homes in Amsterdam.

And there, they must have done some talking and thinking. Because the following market day there was a really shining example of some Amsterdam businessmen talking and thinking.

From Amsterdam came fifteen of the richest businessmen with their shining Cadillacs, Rolls Royces, and similar prestige cars.

They drove right down to the corner fishstore. They parked their big and shiny cars all around the entrances of the fishstore, making a solid blockade! Then they came out of their cars and stepped on the sidewalk in front of the windows, making of themselves also a blockade.

There they were. In their expensive business suits, looking impressive and immaculate. And tough!

The fishman phoned the police for protection. And the police came and asked those businessmen to go away with their cars.

The Amsterdam gentlemen asked very polite if it was a non-parking zone. The police answered that no, it was not that. Then the police asked if they please would not walk in front of the store.

Those Amsterdam gentlemen asked very polite if it was a non-walking zone? No, it was not that either.

The police phoned their superiors for instruction. Then the head of police came down to the fishstore and had the same requests.

One of the businessmen asked, extremely polite, to the head of police: "Do we in any way act unlawful?" The embarrassed head of police had to admit that they were behaving quite correct.

Then those gentlemen smiled at the police, but remained with their cars right in front of that fishstore!

It did not take too long into the night that the fishman gave the jewellery back to Lampel. Everybody came to our hotel. Kibbitzing and celebrating. Because if the police could not help the Jew because of lack of a case, they had made sure that the police could not help the fishman for the same reason.

Those Amsterdam Jews had suffered their losses during the war. Also they had learned a lesson. The lesson was: "We won't take it anymore!"

Gone was the attitude of: "Don't let us make waves."

That had gone with our parents' generation.

But we are here. And for the sake of our children's generation we said: "Not again!"

47

Our Shul

There were so few Jews left in Zwolle that on Sabbath mornings, against Orthodox custom, they phoned around to get *minjan*, the ten men needed to perform some services. Only ten men needed for the only synagogue in Zwolle. Bram was often phoned, and he always went.

We tried to maintain the traditions. Our children learned Hebrew from Mrs. Keizer. When a Purim party was arranged, I dressed Leo and Jack up like cowboys, and Claire and Alida like farmersdaughters, with a kerchief on their hair, wooden shoes on, and a basket with vegetables in their hands.

When it was *Sukkoth*, Mrs. Keizer invited the children to her *Sukkah*, and they came back with apples and sweets. Also, *Simchat Thora* was celebrated. We gave the children each a little bag filled with candies and closed with a bright-coloured bow. I made sure that in each bag were a few candies made of pure sugar. That was supposed to be the tradition. We all went to Shul. There the children got raisins and almonds. For the grown-ups there was delicious buttercake made by Aunt Netje who volunteered. And coffee was volunteered by Mrs. Lampel, who made the best coffee. And that is why I went to synagogue on the holidays. There we met some others. Our friends.

In the women's section, upstairs, there was always a lot of whispering. We got warnings from the *sjammes* (*shammes*, the synagogue caretaker) and disapproving looks from Lampel. But Bram and some of the other men looked up from their prayerbooks and smiled at the women's section, as if they felt happy about us being there.

Good old shul. There was no rabbi. The few surviving Jews came there not so much for religion as to maintain a tradition for the sake of the children. Or maybe just to be together for a few hours. They took turns leading the service.

And there was the responsibility to make it possible to say *kaddish* (memorial prayer) for the ones we had lost. And for the very few deeply religious Jews who had survived, but whose number did not make ten.

Just empty seats.

Empty seats...

48

Showing Our Scars

The children learned to swim. Having to cross a canal by ferry to go to school made me worried, and I let them start young. They became good swimmers.

When Alida did her test, she had to be dressed up, to go fully dressed up in the water. She went in a skirt and had a big, old-fashioned, black, flowered red scarf around her shoulders, and she had some playing cards in her hand. She won first prize as a gypsy fortune teller.

Claire did not like to tread water and stay in the same place. When it was her turn, she wanted to refuse. But her teacher knew her, and when Claire had to jump, the teacher sneaked up behind her and simply pushed her in.

Unfair.

Did nobody notice? There were some smiles around and nobody said anything.

Claire was the youngest of the group. It was fun.

They went to a good school and all four of them did very well.

It bothered us very much that we could not show their report cards to their grandparents or uncles. We could not talk to anybody and boast about their brightness. Just us. They might have thought we neglected it. But that was not so.

Bram and I had to cope with the same feeling. We could never discuss anything with family or ask for advice. We were all on our own.

But we tried to bring up our children in the good values we knew of. And in doing so give them a link with their grandparents and uncles, who would have loved them so much, if they had been allowed to live.

We worked hard, and yes, we were doing well. On Friday cattlemarkets, our restaurant was busy. Also, on the once a month horsemarket, on Thursday.

Bram had nice clubs for his dancing lessons. And the ballroom had during the winterseason the Saturday nights booked for parties.

After the war, we looked all right.

But somehow, sometimes, while not realizing it ourselves, we showed our scars.

In our behaviour.

And sometimes it happened that during a party, when the band played dance music, and the customers laughed and had a good time, and Bram and I were working behind the buffet, Bram handing out to the waiters the ordered drinks and I was filling coffee cups from the big coffee machine, and arranged them on the saucers, that a customer came up to us.

Then the customer asked worried if anything was wrong because we did not smile. We did not realize that. We did not notice we were different from the people around us, who smiled and laughed. Something had changed us, taken something out of us.

We only knew that smiling for us felt strange somehow.

Later on, living in Canada and working, Bram in his job and I in mine, we still were asked: "Why don't you smile?" We had no answer.

We were back in Bram's old familiar surroundings. We were talking again with people Bram knew. And I got to know them too. But sometimes, with a shock, we became aware something had changed for us. Only for us.

That was when people in a conversation mentioned their parents or brothers. Just casual telling about meeting them or talking with them. No matter how casual it was, it did hurt.

Our parents could still have lived. We had no brothers anymore. We would have liked talking with them. But after the war we were different from others. We were outsiders. We missed a sense of belonging.

Bram and I had it very strong. We did not talk about it. Bram might just have mentioned it once. We had never cried for them. But we knew from each other that we became tense when people mentioned their family.

It was still painful.

49

Alida's Surgery

The war was behind us. Life should settle and maybe we would now come to a restful time together. Without fear, without tension.

The children went to school, and Claire and Alida went to ballet lessons, and Leo and Jack to Judo practice. And they would start piano lessons. But rest we did not have yet.

We noticed that Alida had a depression in her breastbone.

We kept an eye on it, but it did not go away. We went with her to Dr. Marcus, our family doctor.

He checked it and told us that if it would stay that way, she might get trouble breathing later on, and he advised us to go to a certain specialist in Utrecht.

The specialist looked at it and told us that it would not improve on its own. He thought there might be an extra connecting bone or muscle that kept front and back together, and had to be removed by operation. There was a problem. It was close to the heart, and the bloodstream from the lungs to the heart had to be stopped so the heart would be clear to reach. Also, the heartbeat might be affected, and it needed a special anesthetic that had just been discovered.

The first operation with that special new technique had just been done in Paris, and Alida would be the second one to be operated with that special method. The specialist,

Dr. Chapchal, would be operating on her in Utrecht at the Academic Hospital. It would be the first in Holland.

We were shocked and afraid.

In Zwolle we went back to Dr. Marcus to ask for his opinion and advice. His answer was simple. He told us there is not a real choice. You might lose her now from the operation. But otherwise she might have trouble breathing later on.

We asked Dr. Marcus what he would do himself. He answered: "If it was my daughter, I would have the operation."

Alida went to Utrecht to the Academic Hospital, and later on somebody brought me after the Friday market to Utrecht. But then I had to go back again to Zwolle. I don't remember how it was all arranged.

For the operation Bram and I went back to Utrecht and heard there that Alida was the second one now in Utrecht. Another child was just recently operated on and was all right. It did not help us to know that and we sat very tense for hours. After the operation we had to go back again to Zwolle.

Bram had that night a big evening affair for a sportsclub in our ballroom. In the middle of the party, while everybody was drinking, eating, and dancing, Bram came up to me and said, "I am restless. I want to go to Alida in Utrecht. Now." I said: "Let us go, then."

Bram went to the leader of the sportsclub, and they were cooperative and promised everything would be run smooth. Bram and I went as we were to our car and drove in the middle of the night to Utrecht.

We were very tense when we walked into the hospital. It was night and it was very quiet. We did not meet any doctors or nurses. We had a terrible fear something might be wrong.

After walking many long halls, we came to Alida's room. It was quiet and we stepped inside. There was Alida, in her bed, sleeping very deep. We just looked at her. She was sleeping, breathing. We left right away her room and walked through all the halls again and came outside.

Then we talked. When she wakes up she should know we were here. She should have something that she would like to play with. And so, in the middle of the night, we went to a big toy store in Utrecht and woke up the owners. Bram asked him to give us the nicest doll he had.

And with the doll back again to Alida's room. Bram did hang it up somewhere, right in front of her, to see right away when she opened her eyes. It was a beautiful doll and had a very sweet face. We hoped it would help her wanting to get better and play with it.

Then, without waking her, or meeting anybody in the halls, we walked out of the hospital again, back to our car, and Bram drove back to Zwolle. In our ballroom the party had finished and everything looked well taken care of. Our waiters had cleaned up and gone home.

Bram was tired. Like so often during the war, he again had made a life-or-death decision.

And I? For many years I told Alida to take care of her doll. I had good feelings for that doll. And Alida?

I'll have to ask her sometime.

50

JAZ—Jewish Amusement Zwolle

There were some Jews in Zwolle that liked to come together socially. They were mostly the parents of young families. Max and Betsy Hony, Eli Content, Bram and me, and a few more. And some old singles like the brothers van Tijn. There were a few more Jews, but they were more on their own. Our little group felt the need for some Jewish activities for our community. That had disappeared with the Jewish majority that had been deported.

So, when we were once as friends together it was decided we should form a club and make cultural or entertaining get-togethers for all the Jews from Zwolle and surrounding towns. We named the club: Jewish Amusement Zwolle. JAZ.

The first thing we did was contact Max Tailleur, who was well known in Amsterdam for his revues and sketches. Max Tailleur came to Zwolle, and our first meeting gave us a shock. Max had an enormous long nose, and was so thoroughly crosseyed that we never could tell who he was looking at.

But when he read the revue for us, we laughed and bought the script. Once a week he came to Zwolle for rehearsals.

To get enough people together, we had to send invitations to some surrounding towns. Two weeks before our date for the show, we received an invitation from one of those surrounding towns to attend their entertainment evening.

We decided to go and rented a bus in which we all went. When we arrived, we saw Max Tailleur. As soon as he noticed us his face turned yellow. When the curtain opened, we knew why. He had sold them the very same revue. We had to depend on the same crowd, and that promised to become a disaster.

In the very first minute of the intermission, we went up to him and explained exactly and in detail what we thought of him. Max kept smiling and remained quite cool. He promised us a new script with new sketches and new songs. And, of course, it would be better than this one.

Someone asked if he expected a miracle? Just two weeks of rehearsals? He promised we would have a better show and it would be great.

Two weeks before the date of the show Max Tailleur came to Zwolle and gave us a completely new revue. Sketches, music, and everything else was new. We started to rehearse just to say our lines. The melodies had to be carried by the musicians because we could not remember everything.

There was one more week left and it was the last rehearsal with Max Tailleur. This time it was Max who attacked one of us.

Betsy Hony, who was one of the performers on stage, had come to rehearsal with all her teeth extracted. Max walked up to her and acted nonchalant. He told her that he had noticed that there was something missing in her head. Betsy ignored the double meaning of that remark, was very cool, smiled at him, and told him that the next week on the evening of the performance she would have a mouth full of beautiful new teeth, but that Max still would be crosseyed. Max looked superior at her and told her that his crossed eyes looked good on him.

Then he forced us to repeat our lines again and again, and sing the songs, and do the sketches. We did not know exactly what we were doing, but having to do it over and over again made us act as if we knew.

When it was the evening of the show, we all acted nonchalant and bluffed our way through. At one time the stage was empty and all the players were in the dressingrooms. Max Tailleur came up to Bram who was in black eveningwear and Max started to shove Bram to the stage and told him to stay there till the next act was ready. Bram said, "You are crazy, what am I going to do?"

Max whispered through his teeth and said: "Talk!"

And Bram acted as if it was all part of the show, walked to the middle of the stage, smiled, and talked.

We heard the audience laugh and applaud, but we did not know what Bram said.

The show was a success, and afterward Bram was leading the ball. Nobody wanted to go home, but at three o'clock we had to close because that is the law connected with our license.

The whole affair got a flattering write up in the *New Jewish Weekly*.

If I try to find a quality that made this impossible affair a success, I can find only one word: *Gotspe!* (Chutzpah!)

51

Hotel Wijnberg

There were six hotels on the cattlemarket. Our hotel had a pleasant atmosphere. We were busy.

The basic business came from the cattlemarket on Friday morning.

It started early, at about five o'clock in the morning. Bram had the coffee ready, and the cattledealers, butchers, and farmers came in to warm up with a drink. Because the cattle market was mostly busiest in winter (because in summer they worked the land) it was very cold that early.

It could happen that when Bram came downstairs at four thirty in the morning, he found already some farmers sitting in the restaurant, drinking our gin. They said good morning to a surprised Bram and told him they had climbed on the upstairs fire exit, and came in at the second floor. They really felt at home. But they told what they had taken and the bill was paid correct.

The cattlemarket was a meeting place for farmers, butchers, and wholesalers. Buying and selling in their own special way. There were big amounts of money involved. And while arguing about price, the buyer offered a price and backed it up by slapping the hand of the seller. If the offer was not accepted, the seller came with another price, also backing it up by slapping the hand of the buyer. And so prices went up or down, backed up by very fast handslapping. It looked very lively.

When they agreed on a price, they shook hands and came to our hotel, and went into our big open kitchen to settle the deal and pay cash, and had something to eat. After that, again to the market for more business.

We had a big, real open kitchen, and used it to serve food. Soup, meals, meat, chicken, pancakes, or anything that I noticed they liked. Our kitchen was very popular and I needed a help with preparing, and an experienced waiter to serve. Our customers also liked it because, when they exchanged money when they closed their deals, they preferred the slightly more privacy of the kitchen instead of the restaurant in the front.

In the restaurant worked the waiters with gin, coffee, and soup. There was a dumbwaiter I could pass the food through to the front. The business in the restaurant was faster. All morning long our customers ran in and out, wearing their wooden clogs and linen market coats. Sometimes a lost cow came walking in. It was funny how somebody could recognise the cow and knew who the owner was.

At about two o'clock in the afternoon, it stopped. Our customers loaded their cows in their big trailers and went home.

Then our cleaninghelp started to throw pails with warm soapwater and hoses with tapwater on the walls and floor to clean up the restaurant and the kitchen. They had washed dishes and done the bedrooms in the morning. The restaurant was built to take hard use and tough cleaning. The walls were of a beautiful blue-green shining material. It was some sort of stone and had a bubbly shining finish. When the cleaning help had finished, everything sparkled and smelled fresh.

We also had quite a few sportsclubs, bicyclers, walkers, and soccer players who considered our restaurant their meetingplace and used it for parties. Usually on Sundays, because that was their day for sports. With the soccerclub it was always unsure what would happen. If they lost, nothing happened. If they won then they came in about an hour later to our restaurant to celebrate and eat and drink. But we could not buy or prepare anything in advance, and Bram was listening very tense to the radio the whole Sunday afternoon. If they won, then the butcher had to be phoned to bring the meat right away and we needed eggs and bread. A waiter had to come and I had to prepare fried eggs and sandwiches for about a hundred people. All within an hour. They came all at the same time. But it worked out and everybody enjoyed it.

Because our business was built up from so many different parts, and so unpredictable, we needed a big staff. Full- and part-time waiters, cleaningladies, a live-in maid, a live-in girl for the children, a stageboy, a dance assistant, and a woman that came once a week to repair the table linens and bed linens and make some pretty dresses for the girls. Sometimes a chef and a gardener. Bram did not like his payroll, but could not change it. And the business carried it.

Bram was at home.

Bram's parents had the hotel built and it was very solid. It had complete double foundations in case they wanted later to build an extra floor on top. But there was not a real livingroom for the family. One of the rooms upstairs had livingroom furniture, and that was all.

With our family together, Bram wanted a real homelife and a real livingroom. He decided he would build one downstairs, on the ground of the garden, next to the restaurant. And a private washroom. Bram told the builders how he wanted it. He thought of nice details and explained it to them.

Then the builders started to work. When the first stone had to be laid, all four children cemented a first stone to our livingroom.

When it was finished it was beautiful. A window to the garden was glass in lead, the other window had a very wide windowsill for flowers or other pretty things. And a hearth with a marble mantelpiece. And some new things we liked and bought for it. Some little woollen Smyrna carpets for the table and wall. And some copper things we could use and liked. It all made the room warm looking and inviting.

We started to feel good. But it was Bram who made the good moments in our life, and was warm and generous, and wanted to share the goodness with the ones he loved. We, his family, were protected by him. After all those years of fear and restlessness, life became worth living.

We felt good. I think the few years we lived in our hotel belonged to the better years in our lives. Our family was together, we had a home and a good business. And we had friends. Life became worthwhile again.

Until...

Until you read the newspapers. And while I write this I am suddenly shocked by the similarity of the time when I was at home in my parents' business. Again, until you read the newspapers.

52

Partir C'est Mourir un Peu

After a war in the Far East, the Russians came in the news. Stalin had always been purging people he considered not suitable for his purposes. That was his general policy. It became more personal to us when in one of his purges he picked out eleven doctors and accused them of sabotage. All were Jews.

The part of our generation that had survived the war had never lost their scars and fears.

And in Holland the Jews started to whisper again. Antisemitism in Russia! Russia could walk to Holland in days or fly to it in a matter of hours. We remembered too deep how fast and solid the Germans had occupied Holland. And how thoroughly antisemitic they had been.

Some Dutch Jews said that this is just a single instance. Other Jews said, "Never mind! Not again! We are leaving."

And with the last group Bram and I agreed. Long before, we had made up our mind that if there ever again was a threat in politics or a doubt about antisemitism or war, we would not wait and see how it would develop, but take it as a warning to leave.

And now it seemed we had to make that decision. We had lost our older generation, our parents, our contemporaries, our brothers to the Nazis. We did not want to take a risk with our younger generation. Our children. Not just waiting or just risking this time.

Before the war, good business and a comfortable life made people undecided, hesitant to give it up. Everything seemed so uncertain. They waited with their decision. And in the end, it killed them. Bram and I knew that danger and had decided long before how to decide in a similar situation. There were already some young Jews going to Israel. Some families to the States. And again we began to feel uncomfortable. Right or wrong, we were going to leave Holland.

But again, where could we go? Now there was Israel. And the first impulse was, "Let us go there." Bram knew of a group of fifteen young families that wanted to go there too, and wanted to go as a group. They planned to start an orange juice export business. They would buy orange groves and bottle the juice in their own factory.

Everyone that wanted to go with that group had to contribute to become a partner. Some supplied machinery, some supplied money for the purchase of land and the factory. They also needed bottles of a certain shape and size. Bram could supply that.

Bram was also in contact with a South American millionaire who wanted to start a hotel-restaurant in Israel for American tourists. Then the South American would bring in customers with chartered flights. Bram would supply the furniture and then become partner-manager in the restaurant. It was too new an idea for Bram.

And once we had an Israeli promoter in our hotel who wanted to sell homes in Kfar Yedidya. Bram decided to go to Israel and look into the possibilities. When he came back from Israel, he decided against it because of the warm climate. He wanted to go to Canada. Bram thought about going to the States, but that would take longer.

Later on, we heard that the group of fifteen families hit hard times in Israel. They had all invested in the orange juice factory, but could never start business because there was not enough sugar available at that time.

They had given up their homes and businesses in Holland, and now they had lost their money that they had invested for a new life in Israel. Some of the women got a nervous breakdown and they had a hard time to recover from it.

Bram contacted the Canadian consulate and the immigration officials in Holland for information, and to apply. At that time, they were quite demanding. Bram had to prove he could make an independent living. We had to have money and a good knowledge of the English language. They also wanted to check out our political background.

When our background and everything else was checked out and approved, they started a conversation with us in English to find out if we spoke it well enough.

Finally, we got our papers.

Bram then had to sell our hotel that had represented home and a good living since we came out of hiding from the Nazis. It was a big decision to give it up. It had been for years in Bram's family. They had built it.

The years we lived in our hotel were maybe for us the better years. We were home. Bram lived in the place where he had grown up and was well known and well liked. And yet, when the political atmosphere worried him, Bram was ready to give it up to bring us, his family, out of the country into safer surroundings.

We had just finished our beautiful livingroom and did not have much time to enjoy it. To uproot our family again and leave our good home behind.

Bram, more than I, was aware that it might change our place in society for the rest of our lives. Our rest had been so short.

Bram had two buyers for the hotel, who would decide on the same day. The first one who was able to supply the money would be the new owner.

The time was set at nine o'clock in the morning for the first buyer. The second one at ten, and he would pay a better price. But because Bram had given his word that he would hold on till one o'clock for the first one, Bram would not break his word and he would accept the lower offer. Nothing was written down. That was the way business was done in our families while they were living. And now with us. And our word was respected. Our word was as good as a written contract.

At a quarter to nine the phone rang. Bram wanted me to answer it. It was the first buyer, who apologized that he could not come on time. I told him that Bram would keep his word that would bind him till nine o'clock, but that afterward he considered himself free.

The would-be buyer laughed a little and said that a big cash deal would not sell so fast. But I repeated a few times that we would only be obliged till exactly nine o'clock. The man laughed again and said that was, of course, all right. Then he hung up.

At ten o'clock the other buyer came and had the money with him. And so the deal was closed. Completely correct. Bram would have accepted the lower offer if it had been on time.

At about eleven thirty the other buyer came. He was very disappointed, but he admitted that he had not realized there were others. But it had all been completely correct and we were in need of time because of the departure of our boat. We could not afford a long time to deal.

But it had sold fast. The buyers had been eager. Our business, Hotel Wijnberg, had a good name.

Bram had made the condition with the buyer that we could stay in the hotel till the day of our leaving. We had about two and a half weeks left.

Bram told our customers and his sportclubs. The sportclubs made an ornament with their name and sport engraved on it and hands in a handshake, to show their friendship.

Then Bram told our friends, and they invited us to a dinner in a fine restaurant. They gave us a silver cup with the initials JAZ engraved on it, from the Jewish Amusement Zwolle, the club we had been a member of. And we got more gifts.

But we all felt very downhearted when we had to say goodbye.

Partir c'est mourir un peu. To part is to die a little.

Who had made the wisest choice? Our friends who stayed behind together or we alone who left everything for an unknown unpredictable future. Not knowing what the future would bring us, Bram wanted to let us have a good last look at our corner of Europe.

Bram rented a trailer and we all went for a beautiful trip in the neighbouring countries. We went through Holland to Belgium through the Ardennes. It was not easy driving a trailer through the mountains, and Jack and Leo had to jump out often to put stones behind the tires of the trailer if it slid back on the mountain roads.

From there we went to the northern part of France.

But at a certain spot not far from the Swiss border, Bram took the car and went alone to make a side trip to Switzerland. With a good reason.

The Dutch government did not allow money above a certain amount to leave the country. Bram, without even telling me where, had put the excess money in the trailer. When we were out of Holland, and close to the Swiss border, Bram took the car and went alone crossing the border into Switzerland and deposited the money in a Swiss bank, to be transferred to a bank in Toronto.

When Bram came back from Switzerland, we went on to Luxembourg. Along the river Meuse to Diekirch. There we stayed. The beauty there was so friendly and inviting. There were green mountains, not too high, but from where you could look down on the rooftops of the villages in the valleys. There was the river. Not too wide. There were towns with a square in the middle and castles on top of the mountains.

They did not look forbidding, as castles can sometimes do. Visiting and looking around in one, we felt more like guests of the oldtime family than as tourists.

Luxembourg was a very small country. It had small towns with white churches with belltowers. When it was churchtime the bells chimed friendly to invite people to come to church.

This trip gave us a rest between all the changes in our lives. But we had come to the end of our trip and had to go back to Holland. At the Dutch border, the customs officer looked at Bram's passport and grinned, disappointed. He understood the meaning of the Swiss stamp and Bram's maneuver. But Bram had done it!

After we had come back from our trip, we had to prepare ourselves to leave for good. We had maybe our moments of worry, maybe a slight regret, to leave again a familiar life behind. Again to be uprooted from everything we felt good with and cared about. To step into a complete unknown, unpredictable future, on a strange continent, with a different language, without knowing anybody there, or even a place to go to when we arrived. And no idea how to make a living there for a family with four young children.

I know that Bram, more than I, realized the enormous risk he took, and again felt the heavy responsibilities.

I followed Bram and trusted him, and that made it easier on me.

It was our last evening in the hotel. We were sitting in the livingroom.

Suddenly, the phone rang and Bram went to answer it. After a while he hung up and seemed puzzled. I asked him who had phoned, and he told me that it had been a total stranger.

This man had heard that we were leaving for Canada and he warned Bram not to go to Canada. He told Bram he had come back from living in Canada and sold up there to come back to Holland.

Bram told the stranger that he had sold our hotel and was ready to leave the next morning. But the stranger insisted that it was still more important not to leave. He said he had felt obliged to warn Bram that he had found Canada too hard and too difficult. Bram was puzzled, but his mind had been made up to go.

Afterward, we never talked about it anymore.

It was the beginning of the fall of 1953.

The next morning, we went to Rotterdam. Beier, who had been headwaiter for the Wijnbergs for twenty years, and Obbe and Marie, brought us to the boat, the *Veendam*. When we left the shore, we felt tense.

Bram had wanted to go by boat because that gave us some extra time to mentally prepare ourselves for the great change in our lives, while we were looking at the ocean and enjoying the nice meals served aboard.

But that too came to an end.

And finally, it was the last few hours before we had to leave everything familiar behind us.

***

In front of us we saw the Statue of Liberty. A first recognizable outpost of a new world. Every minute it came closer. We gathered our children around us. We picked up our luggage.

And then we had to leave the boat and step on land. On a strange continent and a strange big city, with a different language.

We walked slowly, just looking ahead. And finally, we came on land.

We had arrived in New York.

O, were all people wise,
And willing to do well,
Earth could be a paradise,
Now it is often hell.

—Dirk Rafaelsz Camphuysen (translated from the Dutch)

53

The New World

So, this was New York. From the reading we had done about it, it seemed to answer the mental picture we had formed.

We started to walk away from the harbour. We did not know the way, but Bram realized we had to go more downtown and find a hotel so we could put our luggage down.

Bram went into a telephone booth and phoned around and inquired at a few hotels, and then we took a taxi that brought us there.

After we had our rooms and rested a short while, Bram suggested we should have lunch somewhere. So we went for a walk till we saw a cafeteria and we went in.

It was busy and noisy, but clean, and the food was good. After lunch we became impatient to see more of the city. And we went out. And then, near the door, we got a scare. Two or three men walked up with revolvers drawn and went into the cafeteria. We were glad to be outside. But during that first day it happened two more times that we saw men with guns walking around.

And we started to think that it was true what they told about America. The gangsters and all. Later, when we were a little longer around, we found out that they were men from Brinks, collecting money for safekeeping.

We walked around and looked at the skyscrapers, the busy streets, and the big stores.

And while we were walking, many people smiled at us, and complimented us, saying "nice family" while they were passing by. Father and Mother walking with four young children on Fifth Avenue. In our solid and new clothes, we were obviously no New Yorkers.

We walked in a big park and later Bram took us to Radio City Music Hall. After we had dinner that evening, we went to our hotel to sleep.

Bram had made the first day of a new life, on a strange continent, like a holiday. Bram had an art for living that he shared with his family.

The next day we did a little more sightseeing, and then Bram said suddenly that he wanted to leave the same day. We went to our hotel and picked up our luggage. Bram got a taxi and we went to Grand Central Station.

There, we had to wait quite a while. But we did not get bored. It was very big and very busy and we were quite impressed with it.

When it was time, we went to the platform waiting for the arrival of our train. And then we went in and sat down, glad that for a while we just could sit down, and were on our way to Canada.

We must have fallen asleep because suddenly there was a customs officer standing in front of Bram asking him a few questions. Bram started in a hurry to find all our official papers for the whole family. Passports and quite a few more.

While Bram was still looking, the customs officer smiled at him and told him he did not need all that. Just routine checking if everything was all right. Still smiling, he told Bram that when he was going to live in Canada he could burn all that: "You don't need all this here." Then we got a very relaxed feeling. Canada is a hospitable country. And you are free to travel and discover it.

We started to look, interested, out of the window. We noticed that the houses looked fresh painted and there were gardens in front. Most of those houses had a car in their driveway. The sun was shining and it all looked bright and prosperous.

Finally, we arrived at Union Station in Toronto. We stepped off the train and looked around. Bram had phoned to the HIAS in Toronto and somebody would meet us. But we did not see anybody.

Here we were. Strangers, and alone with our children and our luggage. For a moment the thought struck me: God, what are we doing here? What now?

Bram phoned the HIAS and heard that someone was waiting outside with a car to bring us to a hotel. When we walked out of the station we found him. Right away we were sitting in the car and driving away from the station.

While riding through the city, we tried to get some idea of the place where we were going to start a new life. But it was too much and too fast to get any impression. We were glad when we arrived at the hotel and went right away to our room.

Finally, we could put our luggage down on solid ground after three weeks of traveling by boat, car, and train. We should have gone on to Edmonton. But Bram had checked out about Edmonton and decided against it.

Bram made Toronto our destination.

After we refreshed ourselves and made sure we looked correct, Bram said we should have something to eat in a nearby restaurant. And there we found out the name of the street we were. Spadina. And the restaurant might have been Shopsy.

After we had dinner, we made a short walk and Bram noticed a dairy restaurant where he wanted to have breakfast the next morning. And then we went to our room and to bed. We had come a long way, and everything was new and strange.

What would life here bring us?

We were too tired to think about it and fell asleep right away.

The next morning, we washed and dressed ourselves very nice and correct and went to the dairy restaurant for breakfast. The six of us really must have been obvious newcomers or tourists in the eyes of the people sitting there.

One big-built man came up to Bram and asked where he came from and where he was going with the whole family. And Bram told him that we came from Holland and that he wanted to stay in Toronto.

Then the big man said to Bram: "Come with me." And Bram went. Just like that.

It took a little while before I became panicky. Where did that big strong man take Bram? What was going on? What kind of country and what kind of people were this anyway?

Thank goodness, there was Bram back. Alone, and with a big smile on his face.

Before I could ask him anything, he said: "I have a job! Next door, selling chickens. That man seems to own the place, and he hired me."

We must have had the same thought. Is this the way they do things in Canada? But Bram was happy. And that made it all right for us.

Later in the day Bram brought us a basket full with pears, and I thought that a real extravagance. But Bram told me that was the way they buy pears in Canada. And Bram smiled a little.

54

Starting to Settle

We had been in the hotel for a few days when Bram realized that we should have a few rooms and a kitchen. There was something available in a sidestreet off Spadina, and Bram took it. It was horrible. It was not clean and it was owned by an old woman with a big fellow of a son, who might have had a mental problem. We got no keys and I was scared.

Bram wanted to go to Sarnia to meet a Dutch priest, whom he had to give greetings from Obbe and Marie. And Bram wanted to hear from him some general information about living in Canada.

Bram had to stay away the night. The children were in bed, but I could not sleep out of fear for the big son. When I saw a loose leg under a chair, I took it in my hand and stayed awake all night, holding that piece of wood.

The next day I started to organize the kitchen. When Bram came back, I bought some lettuce, ketchup, potatoes, and kosher wieners, and we had our first homemade meal in Canada. But the place was terrible and soon Bram found an apartment on College Street. On College Street we started to settle. After a while our van with our furniture from Holland arrived, and that made the place more liveable.

Bram went to a school to register the children. After having gone to school for a few days, Leo and Jack told us that their clothes were not suitable. We had bought in Holland the best-quality Harris Tweed plus fours, and they had beautiful velour sweaters. Everything the best quality.

But they told us they were not good clothes. They needed "jeans". I asked them what jeans were. And then we went shopping and they pointed out the blue, cotton pants they needed. I could not believe that it was correct for school, but I bought them. And their beautiful-quality clothes were neglected from then on, and they outgrew them.

Bram had to find a rabbi to teach Leo, whose bar mitswe was coming up.

Bram found a rabbi, and Leo started to study his Hebrew prayers. And it was Bram again who made arrangements with a synagogue where Leo would be called before the congregation to recite his prayers and read his part from the Torah.

Although we had been such a short time in the country, all those things had to be done.

Having been through so much, Bram did not want our children to lose too much in the education we hoped to give them, or estrange them from their ties and traditions of their Jewish background. Bram re-established both right away.

And soon enough it was the Sabbath of Leo's bar mitswe.

That Sabbathmorning we were all dressed up and Leo was carrying his new *tallis* (prayershawl).

Here we were, our small family. No grandparents, no uncles, or any relative or friend. Here we were, in a new country where we knew nobody.

And there Leo stepped up to the front of the synagogue and started to recite in a clear voice the prayers and reading from the Torah. And somehow his beautiful young voice touched everybody while he prayed flawless his part.

After the ceremony many of the listeners came to congratulate us and compliment us on his voice. That was very nice of them and it made us feel good.

Afterward we went home, where I had made a small dinner for just the six of us.

No, there were no grandparents or uncles, so whatever Bram wanted the children to have, he tried to give them.

***

Being the first summer in Canada, we were surprised about the long schoolholidays. To have four young children in a downtown apartment for the summer did not seem right. Bram did not get a holiday from his work and was thinking and inquiring what was possible for the kids. He heard that they might go to a B'nai B'rith summercamp. Bram worked hard at that. He filled out forms, and more forms. And went often to their office, until he finally had made sure that our children would have a summerholiday. I feel that Bram achieved so much the very first year in a strange country. While he himself had to adjust to a different lifestyle.

On parents' day we went to Haliburton and then Bram took the kids, and we all went for a picnic.

Jack, who is not a full year younger than Leo, then had to start to study for his bar mitswe. Jack went to a class with other boys of his age and had a difficult time, being a newcomer.

They teased him and snitched little tales. An inexperienced teacher listened to their snitching. In their old school, and in our home, snitching was discouraged. Jack told us, but we did not know how to deal with that.

Jack himself found the answer.

One day, after another undeserved reprimand from the teacher, Jack spoke up. He asked the teacher why he did not pay those little snitchers the Judas penny they deserved. That was what the teacher in his old school did with snitchers.

The teacher became red in the face and changed his attitude.

And then it was the Sabbath of Jack's bar mitswe.

We heard the clear voice of our younger son recite the prayers and the reading from the Torah with a feeling that involved the listeners. It would have been beautiful if their grandparents and uncles would have lived and could have been there to make our sons feel special and give them presents.

Instead, our sons gave to us.

A feeling of pride and hope.

***

After we lived for a short while on College Street, Bram started to think about improving on his job. One day he told me he could become nightmanager in a restaurant. At the same time the owner of the chicken business told him he was opening a store at the new Lawrence Plaza and he could become a manager there.

Bram asked me what I thought was better. I did not want to make the decision for him because it was important that he liked what he did. After all he was the only breadwinner. And day after day I tried to find out what he liked the best, without giving him a definite opinion.

Finally, he came to the conclusion that he wanted to work in the restaurant because his background of his own business would make him feel better. He was used to deal with a large staff. In our own hotel we had at least twenty-two people on the payroll.

So Bram started in his new job and worked in it as if it was his own business.

But what we did not realise then was that it would always be nightwork.

We lived in an apartment with the six of us. Bram worked at night in the restaurant and I was home with the children. Sometimes, if I could not sleep, I went downstairs, walking around till I saw Bram coming. Then we went both upstairs and talked a short time about our experiences of that day. But we did not keep that up. We needed our sleep.

Then one day Bram told me he wanted to move out of this old neighbourhood and give us better surroundings. We looked for an apartment more to the north of the city. But while everybody complimented us about our children, landlords and landladies slammed the door in our faces. Too big family they said. We did not understand their attitude. But it forced us to look for a house to buy.

We found a small house that seemed all right for the time being.

The one thing that made us decide for it was the big backyard where the children could play without the dangers of cars. There were swings in it, and we asked the owners if they would leave the swings there when they moved out.

They said yes. I felt happy that our children would have something to enjoy after all the changes they had to make. But when we moved in, the swings were gone. When Bram inquired about it, the answer was that it had not been written down.

Why was it necessary to write down a toy in a contract? Was their promise not good enough? To us, who were used to more reliable ways in business, it seemed downright dishonest. I felt they had cheated our kids. We were "green" and they had been "smart."

And their word did not mean much.

55

Hurricane Hazel

We moved in. We put most of our furniture in the basement. We had brought from Holland all our favourite things, to surround us here as a help against homesickness because it was so familiar to us. Our furniture and tablesilver and linen. Our woolen blankets. Good paintings and all our books. Even our bone china dinner and breakfast sets and some hotel dinner settings, meat plates, and soupterrines. Then there had been a bed from Max. We could not take it with us but I just could not leave it behind. We decided to sell it and buy with the money a big silver soup-serving spoon and consider it a gift from Max.

Now most of it had been put in the basement. We wanted to distribute it gradually through the house and find the right place for it.

It was only in the basement for a few days when it suddenly got ruined. Something we had never experienced before happened. Hurricane Hazel.

While we were looking unbelieving through the windows, and heard the unfamiliar strength of the storm, and saw the rain come pouring down, in the basement there was water backing up from the ground and came almost shoulderhigh, covering everything that we had storaged there. We had the lowest basement in the street and were completely flooded.

When we noticed what was happening, Leo and Jack went down and tried to save whatever they could carry. It was a terrible job to work in all that water. They worked hard.

Bram was at his new job and felt obliged to work for his boss before thinking about his own losses.

It was a sad beginning. So many nice things that had come all the way from Holland to make us feel here at home were ruined.

So many of our good books we had were rotted by water and had to be thrown out. It was a setback. Emotional and financial.

But we could not stand still with it. Work had to be done, bills had to be paid. We looked later on for another house but were already in the routine of paying the mortgage. Or maybe another job for Bram with no night work. But Bram felt the responsibilities for his family and paying all the bills. So we took it in our stride and went on working, living, paying.

Once I persuaded Bram to let me try a chance on an independent way of making a living.

We started a children's wear store. Bram had not much confidence in it, but he let me try it. We invested whatever we had left and paid cash for most of the merchandise. But the style of doing business here was different than the correct and sincere way the Dutch suppliers treated the bona fide shopkeeper. Also, there was a panicky feeling about what to do if, heaven forbid, one of the children turned sick. Stay home and close the store. I could not handle it. It made us broke.

Bram could have blamed me, but never did he mention the store or the loss of money.

I found that very special of him and respected him for it. His character.

We sold out to jobbers and they asked me if I would mind being employed by them and selling our own merchandise, which they had bought from us.

After our loss I was glad to get a job and said right away yes.

After about four weeks the store was practically empty. I must have done a fairly good job because they asked me if I wanted to do another liquidation.

And so from one store to the next, always about four weeks, I did a big number of sell-offs and liquidations over seven years.

I felt a responsibility about the money we had lost in our store, and tried to be useful.

While working for those jobbers in one of the sellouts of a ladieswear store, I had something happening to me that reminded me of my experience with a Nazi that I had in Holland in our own store.

This sale was somewhere in Bloor Street. One day a big man comes in with two rather heavy-built women. I told them that they could look around and could ask me for a reduced price because it was a liquidation sale. Suddenly the man talked very aggressive to me in a German accent. Why did I not have the reduced price on the articles? I explained there was no time or help enough for that. But he did not give up. He went on in a harsh way, also insinuating about Jews owning the store. The women he had with him tried to quiet him down. They seemed embarrassed.

But he liked to bully again, like the antisemitic bully he must have been during the war.

So far I had spoken English. But suddenly I changed into German and told them to leave. The women were shocked and became uncomfortable. That I understood them made them feel exposed as the Nazis they must have been. I went on in the German language that this was Canada and I would call the police.

I made it clear to them that the positions had changed and if I called the police they might be exposed as Nazis and be illegal in Canada.

They left the store. But to me the victory came too late because it could not save anybody anymore. And it still made me feel shaky. But I realized that was left from the past.

I was upset and went to my next-door neighbour who had a grocery store. He had been in a concentration camp in Europe. I told him what had happened to me and he was terribly sorry that I had not called him. But I could not have left them alone in the store.

The neighbour gave me the advice that, if they ever came back, I should step on the men's toes, and if he would try to push me away, I should call for help and accuse him of attacking me. The neighbour would have preferred to come and help me, and the way he reacted showed a long-time bitterness.

56

Finding Our Place

Before we left Holland to go to Canada, Bram and I had talked about how in the future we could keep our children free from the dangers of antisemitism. And we came to the conclusion that when we arrived in Canada we would not tell people that we were Jews. We wanted to blend in with the gentile population. And our children would grow up fitting in with the majority.

After we were a few days in Toronto, Bram discussed with a Canadian Jew.

The Canadian said we would also have to change our name because Wijnberg sounded Jewish. Besides that, he did not think it necessary. There were enough Jews in Canada that we would not feel helpless or uncomfortable. And, indeed, where we started, at Spadina, we saw so many Jews around, and kosher restaurants and butchers, that we decided it was all right to be Jewish here.

And we enjoyed the atmosphere. Something we had lost in Holland and we thought did not exist anymore.

But still we were alone. These Jews had lived here for many years and were with their families and had their own friends already. We were newcomers, outsiders. And they never really understood what the war had done to us. Our loneliness. That it can happen where Jews live.

Of course, they "knew" all about what had been going on during the war. They had read it in the newspapers. The same papers that gave stockmarket information and had sportsnews on the front page. Having escaped the concentrationcamps during five years of war was not so important.

Soon enough we stopped talking, stopped trying to tell. It reminded me of the time that the Dutch Jews could not identify with the German Jewish refugees because they seemed different.

But the Dutch Jews assisted them from the moment they came off the train. Because they were Jews just like we were, and our lives became later intertwined with theirs. We learned that to an antisemite there were no dividing lines of countries.

We were all Jews.

It took the Canadian Jews many years and movies and books to give them an idea about the big crime that had been committed to the European people that were Jews, as they were.

But by then we did not want to talk about it anymore. We did not want to be reminded.

Just our family should know. Should know why they did not have grandparents and uncles. Should know that they had been loving and cultured people. Our children should be proud of their roots.

And we were hoping that our children may understand that we could not be easygoing or smooth-talking like their friends' parents. We had a different background and could not communicate because our life experiences were so different. It made us feel lonely. And misunderstood. But now we did not try to tell anymore. We were just too tired.

Although our war experiences and our emigration had made us tired, we were still not excluded from the worries and sicknesses that happen in most families with growing children.

Jack, who had a paperroute, had a fall while delivering papers. He went to a house where they phoned Bram to pick him up from and Bram phoned me at work and I came home.

Bram put Jack in the car and the three of us went to our family doctor. Who did nothing! Gave no first aid or any attention. All he did was phone a doctor in a hospital.

There we were, waiting with Jack bleeding till he finished his phone call and then we had to go to this hospital where Jack got some stitches just above his eye. Thank God, it came out all right.

Then Claire had trouble with her legs, and after a few months trying at night her legs in a cast, a doctor advised an operation. We were extremely worried. We could certainly not talk to our family doctor who was so uninvolved.

Bram wrote to Utrecht to the specialist who had operated on Alice (Alida) and Bram asked that specialist how he would do the operation and explain it to the doctor who would do the operation here.

The specialist answered right away and made a diagram and gave his advice to the surgeon here. We did not know if he accepted the Dutch surgeon's suggestions.

It was different from our feelings when Alice had her operation. On the day of Claire's operation Bram and I were extremely tense. We were more afraid because we could not discuss anything with anybody.

Thank God, it was a success. She came home but had to recover in bed for some months. Her neighbour and girlfriend came often and brought some schoolwork.

And when it was Christmastime Bram took her for an evening trip in the car and showed her all the lights and Christmas decorations.

But it had been difficult time, and I am sorry that I escaped by going to work. Bram was home till four thirty, Leo came home at four o'clock, and after six I came. But I am sorry till this day that I did not stay home.

Bram worked hard. Every night. He left the house at four thirty in the afternoon and came back at night at three thirty. I worked during the day. That was not good for the children, not good for Bram and me, not good for homelife. But working and being tired, and having to sleep, Bram during the day, me during the night, we had no time or energy to discuss a change. We carried on. When Bram came home at night, he often brought fresh bread or cookies for the children for breakfast or to take to school.

Every week Bram took me to a movie that was new and considered good. Bram also took sometimes the children if he could. With him we saw *Around the World in Eighty Days* and *Lawrence of Arabia*. Also we went together to the Theater in the Dell for *O, Coward*, with Kneebone and Christie. Also, a vacation with the boys in Atlantic City while the girls were with Selma in Connecticut. And we had once a nice holiday in a rented cottage in Huntsville. And always a drive on Sunday.

Bram lived and worked for his family and gave them all he could.

But something was missing in our lives. Family or old-time friends. The kind of people you could discuss your plans with or changes you might like to make. Or the kind of people that would have been concerned about our unending workload. The workshifts that kept us apart. Bram tried once to change the hours in his job, but met with such strong refusal that he even might have worried about even keeping his nighttime job. When it was too late for us, I heard for the first time the expression "graveyardshift." Bram carried the responsibilities for his family of six people, for the mortgage, the taxes, the food and heating, and all kinds of other bills. He must have worried, and in his job they might have made him feel cornered. Too many years devoted to one place. And nobody to encourage him or be supportive to him in helping him find a way out of his routine.

I could not. I was too much like him. I shared the same feeling of fear and worry. We both had a sense of insecurity. During the war, when we never were sure that we would wake up the next morning in the same place that we went to sleep the evening before, had given us both a lack of confidence. Confidence that you need to plan for the future.

In Holland in our own business, and surrounded by some good friends, we felt stronger. But here we could not communicate with anybody. We remained outsiders. The language had never been a barrier. But our different backgrounds were. Even our sense of humour was different, and we even had to keep that to ourselves because we were misunderstood.

Bram was satisfied to work and provide for his family. But his health could not accept the long, late at night hours.

Daytime sleep is not as restful. But Bram went on.

Sometimes I think that if Max, my brother, would have lived, he would have been concerned about us and might have changed Bram's attitude or start a business with him. Or just make Bram aware of our lonely lifestyle. Maybe our old-time friends. One of them, Herman Melkman, phoned us from Holland. Alice was there on her way back from Israel, and he phoned to tell that she was there, and that he would like to give her a job. And that Bram and I should leave Canada, come back to Holland, and become partner with him in a gambling casino he had in Germany. He told Bram there was money enough for all of us.

Bram and I had experienced the same fears, the same losses, and it made us both worried about more changes. The same lack of confidence, the worry for the future. It made us hesitate about more changes. Bram and I were much alike.

We had the same worried outlook on life. I had no courage of my own anymore and Bram had become too tired. We had no different plans or ideas that might have changed things. If we would have been more different in our opinions and feelings that would have given a reason for discussion, we might have come to a change.

57

Nightmares

There were the nightmares. Many survivors had them. Bram suffered them quite often. Waking up from them he was in a cold sweat. He then told me he had had a nightmare. I did not ask what about. I did not realise it was part of being a victim of surviving. I had only a few, just recently. I had one last night, and remember Bram having them. I know now more about it. Waking up from one, there is fear and heartbeatings and again fear. There is no explanation or reason possible like there might be with some dreams. Just terror. About being followed by Nazis, without seeing them. Going from strange place to strange place.

The strongest feeling for me was of being separated of someone I loved. Pa, Mom, Max, or Bram. I did not see their faces and did not feel their presence. I was separated from them by a danger they were in and not being able to reach them.

I woke up in a grey light and was afraid to stay in bed, and too afraid to get up. The feeling of fear is still active and my heart beats too strong. As if I had been running.

This was one of my few nightmares. Bram had suffered them more often. It makes you feel small and helpless and lonely and scared of something. It cannot be explained.

Although we did not understand the connection, it is part of surviving the killing of your loved ones. I think as a survivor it is possible to receive compensation for it, although you cannot prove to suffer from it. But I am not sure of that because we never asked for it.

During our hiding out, I had a nightmare how my parents and Max had been followed by the Nazis. I wanted to see them and warn them. In my nightmare I asked in different places if they were there. But they always had just left. When I came finally to the last house, my family had just been taken by the Nazis. I was just too late. What I had dreamed about them was very close to the reality. I still remember how helpless I felt.

Or the nightmare in which my father was separated from everybody and let down alone in a deep and dark saltmine. I wanted to see and talk with him and tried to get down in the mine too. But I never could reach him. He disappeared in the darkness at the bottom of the mine. These were just my few nightmares. Bram suffered more.

But it had been just nightmares. The reality was probably concentrationcamp Sobibor. A death camp.

58

Remembering Our Roots

I wrote this for our children. To let them know about their roots. They knew their dad and their mother. But could not possibly place them within the generation of their grandparents. Because I knew that in the thirty years that I lived here, nobody ever mentioned the name of my parents or brother. I was painfully aware of that, and still hoped maybe for the impossible.

Only once, while working in a store, I heard a couple talk Dutch, and I made it known that I could understand, but that I did not want to listen in.

Then, after talking a little longer, we discovered that the man's father had been a supplier of merchandise for my father. The son now owned a factory with forty staff in California, but he did not like the way business was done there. Bram told him about our two children's wear stores here and that we had the same feeling.

The son and his wife were here visiting from the States where they now lived. While they were here, they invited Bram and I to come and visit for an evening.

Bram and I did go.

We talked, but did not ask each other what had happened to the families. We talked with them about the past. About our parents. Very personal. Then, reliving that time, he said in a soft faraway voice: "Did you know that your father had unlimited credit?" And I told him that his father's correct ways in business was well known.

Then the conversation stopped. We sat quiet. We had said all we wanted to say.

We felt strange now in this country where nobody knew those people who had existed, who had been respected, and had once been important to their surroundings. Our parents. And our brothers.

We are alone now and live only on the surface. We do not belong. We have no roots anymore.

Because nobody knew our parents!

Years later I suddenly remembered that it had been his sister who was married to the German refugee and lived in Utrecht. And that they, to escape the Nazis, had committed suicide while she was six months pregnant.

59

Leo and Sheila, Claire and David

Later on, Bram and I went on trips together. Bram made it a habit to phone home from where we were, to hear if everything was all right and talk to the children.

One time, when Bram phoned from Montreal, Jack answered and told Bram that he, Jack, was going to be best man at a wedding. Bram said, "That is nice. Who is getting married?" And Jack answered: "My brother Leo is."

We were dazed, we did not believe it, and asked for Leo to come to the phone. And Leo confirmed it. Then we thought, "Well, that will not be for some time."

But we were invited that same weekend for dinner, to meet the family. We had to give up our holiday plans and went to meet his girl for the first time. When we went home, we had to get used to the idea that our oldest son was a man and going to be married soon.

The date was set. 30 January 1965. Alice and Claire were going to be bridesmaids. Time went fast.

When Bram and I went to pick up their bridesmaid dresses, I opened the box in the car to see what they had decided on. I did not like them, and we went back to the manufacturer to ask if he could improve on it.

He was very helpful and made some changes in just one and a half days. And then we brought them to a well-known fashion designer who helped out by beading them a little. All in record time.

The wedding was nice and everybody looked fine.

After Leo's wedding Claire began dating her escort when she was a bridesmaid. He was a nice young man and Claire seemed to have a good time.

So we did not give it much thought.

One day, after she went out to the car with him, she came back a few minutes later, flashing a ring. We thought that was a beautiful gift, but too expensive. It did not even occur to us that this was the announcement of their engagement. And the young man, David, phoned from our home his parents and told them over the phone: "I am going to marry Claire." And that was the first time we heard about that. Bram and I were again taken by surprise. David and Claire seemed particularly young. But they acted so efficient. They made an appointment with a photographer. And David wanted a special band for the music at their wedding. All we could do was watching how two young people took the lead in their own lives.

Bram and I were invited by David's parents to their house for dinner. After we had tea, the date was set, the synagogue chosen, and even the menu for the wedding was discussed. We wanted a nice wedding for them.

We had a smile when David's parents met Bram for the first time and looked at Bram's bright-red hair. And then they looked at Claire's red hair and said: "It is real! You have it from your father."

The wedding was a very nice affair and everybody enjoyed it.

After dinner David made a speech, thanking his parents and wondering why not everybody could go home then, because he wanted to leave with Claire for their honeymoon right away. He did not care for more dinner.

Aside for some lighthearted booing, the speech of the groom was received with laughter and applause. And in the following years, David's family and ours became friends and grew closer together.

60

Jack and Ida

Time did not stand still. Neither did our children. They made decisions and we did not always feel comfortable with their plans. Jack quit university for a year and left home and worked. After about a year he went back to university.

One day Jack came in and told us he wanted to make a trip to Europe. A friend of his, visiting him, told Jack not only to go to Europe but also to Japan. The world fair was there. Jack thought that a great idea. And he started to make plans for his trip.

Bram and I were really worried. Young people with little money, in strange countries, have not much choice about the company they might get thrown together with. But like many parents in a situation like that, there is not much you can do but go along.

Jack asked me if I would mind to make a going away dinner for him the next Sunday.

Of course I would do that.

And as if on second thought he asked if he could bring a girl he knew for dinner. And again our answer was yes.

So I made a dinner. Alice came, and Leo and Sheila and Claire and David.

And Jack and a girl.

After we had dinner and tea, Bram and I brought Alice back to her apartment. And then we went back home. We were quiet. Thinking about Jack leaving us.

When we came back in our house, there we saw Jack sitting on the couch and in front of him, on the table, a bottle of wine and two glasses. And I asked: "Well, Jack, are you getting drunk or something dumb like that? Why a bottle and two glasses for you?"

With a grin he said: "I just drank to my engagement to Ida, the girl you had for dinner."

After congratulating him, Bram and I had the same thought. Japan is out.

Soon enough it was Jack's wedding day. What I remember most of all was the speech Jack made. It was beautiful. He compared a Jewish young man marrying a Jewish girl like a homecoming again. Not losing one home, but a home of his own to carry on. He said it better and he said more. His words touched everybody's heart. And most guests had tears in their eyes.

Bram and I, being the parents of our two sons, Leo and Jack, having seen them grow into good men, we have been through highlights of our lives, when our sons as babies had their brith hamilos, as young men their bar mitswes, and when we saw them as men under the goupah.

We had to let them go then and wish them God's blessing on their own road.

Jack, our son was married. Jack who as a young child had been hidden from the Nazis by the family van Brummelen in Holland.

Many years later, Jack made a big trip and travelled from Canada to the Far East. On his way back he travelled in Europe and went to Holland to visit the van Brummelens. And there van Brummelen told him that he had always hoped to see Jack back as an adult, before he died. And he embraced Jack.

When Jack was back in Toronto, he received after a short while a card from van Brummelen's widow to tell Jack that her husband had passed away.

Strange how life can sometimes end when one's living is in balance.

61

Alice and Alan

Then there was Alice. Working in an office and living in an apartment that she shared with an English girl that seemed to keep her busy.

Once, when I went to visit Alice and brought her a jacket, she introduced me to a young man. Alan. When I went home, I was wondering if the jacket would fit her, and I hoped she would like it.

I never knew if she liked the jacket, but about a few weeks later she came home with Alan and they told us they were going to get married. Surprises like that we had with our three other children, and so Alice was just keeping the trend.

Soon after that, we were invited by Alan's mother for dinner. It was beautiful. His mother had put so much effort in that meal. I don't remember what we ate, but it must have been delicious.

There was a small wedding. After the ceremony, we went to a very good hotel, and Bram had instructed (with money!) the maître d' how he wanted it.

It was a very nice and intimate dinner, with very good service. There was also a band in the next room, and the young couple and the others could dance.

We all felt happy and comfortable.

And Bram and I had the simcha that we had seen our daughters grow up, and had brought them under the goupah.

Bram felt good and so did I. Our family would go on.

It was right.

62

Tradition

There were the Jewish holidays which Bram continued to celebrate in the old tradition. We had dinner with our whole family gathered around the table. Our two sons and our two sons-in-law, and our two daughters and our two daughters-in-law. And our lovely grandchildren. Everybody looked so nice.

New Year's, Bram started the meal with the blessing for the bread and apple and honey. And after the short prayer he handed everybody a piece of bread and apple and honey, and wishing that the coming year would be for everybody as sweet as apple and honey together. Then we had dinner with wine to start off the new year sweet and right.

Ten days later we had everybody for the breakfast after Yom Kippur. On Yom Kippur, the Day of Atonement, everybody fasted.

They all went to synagogue, and when it became evening, they came gradually wandering in. Some had a headache, but Bram could fast a full day without too much discomfort.

I had the table set, and coffee and tea ready. I liked them to have Dutch rusks that would be a soft start for the empty stomach. But there were all kinds of other things. There was raisin challah and coffee with whipped cream. There was salmon salad and herring. Dutch honeycake, fruitbread with icing, different cheeses, and homefried potatoes, or sometimes homemade fishcakes. The table was set to overflowing. But I should not forget anything because it would be noticed.

Nobody needed to be invited. To break the fast at our home was a tradition.

Chanukah. The festival of hope and light and gift giving. Bram bought for all the grandchildren toys in a special toyshop he favoured. I often thought that they were some toys he might have liked to have himself when he was a child. I did the shopping for their clothes. Once a year we could choose for them.

When the evening of the party was there, all the grandchildren gathered around, and starting from the oldest, they all would light a coloured candle, and we could see the light softly reflecting in their eyes.

Bram said the prayer for light and sang the traditional song. And we sang along with him.

After that we had dinner. The grandchildren wanted to get it fast over with because after dinner they were getting their presents. But when I started dinner with boiled meat soup and celeryroot salad and hot French stick, they must have been eating, because it all disappeared.

Because we could not keep up with the birthdays of the parents, and their anniversaries, instead we gave them a gift at Chanukah.

The grandchildren who had unwrapped their toys and clothes, and their parents who had unwrapped their gifts, left there quite a pile of wrapping-paper on the floor. I admit it was not very organized and it looked quite messy. Bram gave the grandchildren also their initial in chocolate, which they ate in record time. It was in Holland the custom to give each other a chocolate initial on St. Nicholas Day, and when Bram started to give it here on Chanukah, the grandchildren thought it a good idea to make it a Canadian Chanukah tradition. And then we escaped back to the diningroom.

Unbelievable how fast our grandchildren could be. There they were already, having their mouths full, while they were looking with the eye of connoisseurs what to choose. That was an easy choice. They wanted everything.

There was appletorte, sometimes orange chiffon pudding or fruits. Every holiday had some special foods. And from a big bowl of dairy whipping cream that I had on the table, they covered everything with lots of whipping cream. And so did their parents.

I did not hear the word "diet."

Pesach. A very special night was when the Passover story was told. Bram gave the Seder in Hebrew. There he was, sitting on his chair at the head of the table and with two pillows to lean on. After the blessing for the wine had been said, Bram pointed to the matzo and started to tell the story of the Exodus from Egypt, beginning with the words: *Holachmo Anjo* (*Ha Lachma Anya*), "This is the bread of misery".

Then one or sometimes two grandchildren asked him what made this night so different from all other nights. Bram answered by reading the whole story in a Hebrew singsong, changing into the different tunes belonging to certain parts. The old singsongs and tunes he must have heard from his father.

He often stopped to explain in English about the different kinds of people. The wise one. Or the contrary one, who takes a distance of the others by asking, "What does this mean to you?" And Bram quoted the different rabbis that were mentioned. Bram was knowledgeable and made it interesting. And every story he gave their own melody and so he sang the whole Seder and often explaining in English what happened to the Jews long ago.

Halfway, Bram laughed and said: "Now we are going to eat."

The dinner I made also became traditional. The vegetable soup with the solid matzoballs, sometimes stewed chestnuts, and some vegetable. And for dessert always the sweet matzocookies, *gremselich*, with raisins and almonds. And the compote from dried fruit. Every year the same. I hoped they liked the cooking, but I would not have changed it, because that also became a form of tradition.

We could bensj.

After dinner we joined Bram in the familiar songs with melodies you remembered from one year to the next.

It was a beautiful service and now it still hurts to miss him this special night. We hoped that our children realized the value of their roots that we tried to give them.

After we lost Bram, I was invited to celebrate the holidays with our children. If there is a hereafter, Bram will smile and feel good to see all our children, our whole family, sit around a nice set table and carry on the good things in life he had tried to give them.

Thank you, Bram.

Thank you, children.

63

Ik heb je lief

Now Bram and I were alone. And because our responsibilities towards our children became lighter, Bram and I should have enjoyed. But something did not change. And that was our working habits. We did not feel secure enough to do less.

We should have sat down and take stock and make plans. We did not. We carried on a workload that had been a burden for years.

Looking back on our lives, the Depression, the war years, our hiding out with so many dangers and losses, and all the things we had experienced, we should have known better. Our emigration with four young children, starting a new life in strange surroundings and only ourselves to depend on, we should have tried to change our lifestyle.

But years of adjusting, conforming, being forced to fit in, took its toll on our independent way of thinking and our self-knowledge. The drain and strain of all those years of hard work had emptied us mentally and physically. Bram, who had carried the biggest burden, became tired and weak. And afraid to give up his job after so many years. I know that they made him believe that all those years of hard work and loyalty would be compensated with security. That was a lie.

I did not understand what was happening. We became both quiet. Bram became sad.

Now I understand, finally, and I am sad.

We always were almost too much alike to be able to take a distant look and see what happened to the other.

We could not compare because it happened to both of us.

After some misunderstanding, Bram once said: "We are from the same background." The same background or roots, indeed. But what did he try to tell me? I did not understand him anymore. I was unhappy but tried to wait it out till our retirement. We did not understand each other anymore. Or maybe I had turned away, had enough of waiting. We both lost.

But Bram, all through his life, gave the best of himself. Especially to those he loved. His family. And me, his wife.

I became difficult. I saw Bram suddenly turn old and my reaction was anger. I might have felt his life slipping away from me and I did not want to cope with it. Bram was trying to reach out for help from me and did not find the right way either. Sometimes he asked me, "Jetje, wat moet ik?" (Jetje, what am I going to do?) And I did not understand him and did not know what he was referring to. And I did not answer him.

It had taken so many years, and too hard work and so little rest together, that made two loving people lose communication in a time it was so desperately needed.

And then the last Saturday came. Bram did not feel well. I asked him whether I should stay home from work. He answered no, because he would rest up and then would feel better. And I said to him before I left for work, "I will try to come home an hour earlier and see you before you leave. Is that OK? Yes?" And he said something that he would rest up and that he had to go to work in time because his boss was in Florida.

At work I asked if I could go home at four o'clock instead of six. "Maybe" was the answer. When it was not busy, I asked if I could go at three. And that was all right.

At three o'clock I was ready to go home, when I got called to the phone.

It was Bram, and he said: "I go to the hospital. I go by ambulance."

I shouted: "I am coming home!"

I ran out of the store and heard a breaking noise. It was my coffeecup that had broken in my shopping bag. While I was running, I threw out the pieces in a garbage container. I thought: "This is a bad sign."

I drove home faster than I ever drove in my life.

When I came home, I saw Bram had blood on his face and was perspiring and looked helpless.

He had fainted and fallen and had hurt his face.

I did not know what to say or what to do, and the ambulance came before I thought of something. And while I was there, Bram looked at me and said: "Tonight, the boss is not in, but Monday I am not going back to work."

And for one fleeting instant I was happy and I knew that had to be the best thing to happen. He had made the decision himself.

We wanted time and rest together.

Bram was carried away into the ambulance, and the ambulance drove away. And I ran to my car and wanted to go right after him. The neighbours wanted to stop me and drive me to the hospital.

But I wanted to follow right away with my own car.

When I arrived at the hospital, he laid in a little emergency room with some monitor that showed the heartbeat. It did not look very strong and my heart tightened up.

And then they would phone the doctor and the specialist. But nobody came. Bram told me he had massive pain. And I asked for a painkiller and phoned Leo.

And Leo came, and Claire, and Selma and Chaim.

Leo insisted the specialist should come and Bram needed intensive care. He phoned a few times. While Leo was on the phone, I said to Bram: "You have fine children." Bram looked up at them and seemed to feel right about them.

This hospital had no bed free in intensive care, so Bram should go to another hospital.

And Bram made me a diagram and gave me the streetnames how I could come there. I said to him, "You are always the best in helping me to find the way."

When I saw an ambulance come, I went in my car and started to drive to that other hospital.

After I waited there a while, and Bram did not come, I phoned to the first hospital. And they told me he would stay there and had a room in intensive care. So I drove back fast.

I went up in that old hospital and saw Bram lying in a room upstairs. Not a very pleasant room.

There still had been no doctor and no specialist. But there was a nurse in a connecting room, who could look in from behind a glass wall.

I was with Bram. He told the nurse he should have his medicine, Inderal. The nurse said, "OK, in the next hour you will. Would you like a cup of tea?"

Bram said yes, he would like that.

She told me that he was resting comfortably now, and she gave me the feeling I should go.

I said to Bram, "I think she wants to get rid of me, that I have to go now."

And then, while I was standing next to him, he looked at me and he gave me a little stroke up my arm with an encouraging smile on his face. I said, "*Ik heb je lief*" (I love you). And he answered with his smile, "*Dat weet ik*" (I know that). We said it in Dutch. Our childhood language.

And then I left.

I was not home too long before some doctor phoned me it was over. And I shouted "Nooo, Nooo!"

I went back to see him. His face showed pain.

And I kissed him, once.

And so it began, forty years ago, that a red-haired young man stroked my arm, and that we fell in love.

And forty years went by of our lives. Our engagement and marriage. Forty years went by of living and making mistakes. And suffering losses. We have known fear and despair. And we brought up a family of four children.

It was not an easy life.

But it was meaningful, in the fulfillment of human beings. Marriage, man and wife. Two good sons and two good daughters.

And lovely grandchildren. We did not fail.

And now again Bram had stroked my arm. It had been our first and last touch in our life together. It meant "I love you," and we looked in each other's eyes. But now I was losing my home there.

Bram and my life together had come to a full circle. We had exchanged our "I love you" for the last time.

Later on, I gathered some dried flowers that had been included in a bouquet of live flowers, which he gave me on our last anniversary.

And when I put them together, I saw that they were white with green, like a bridal bouquet. And some dark purple ones, as a colour for death.

Bram had never given me dried flowers before. Always live flowers. And I know that he watched my reaction when I noticed them in the bouquet.

There was a message in your last gift to me. Flowers of love for your bride and widow. From Bram, my husband.

Maybe I had to stay behind and tell our story. If our fate would have been reversed, Bram would have written it.

Because our children should know their roots.

Epilogue

You cannot judge a generation, or people, by their vocabulary. But maybe you can by the way they use the same words. In the generation I grew up in, they used the same words, but they had a different meaning. For instance, "liberated" in our generation meant that you were free of fear for your life. Now, "liberated" is connected with the new way people behave, free from duties, or sometimes free from shame.

In the generation I grew up in, "to escape" meant you were able to run away from prison or death. Now "escape" means you detach yourselves from your everyday chores in something more to your taste.

And some words from our generation don't mean anything to the now people.

For instance, "displaced person," or "DP," is just a word without particular hurt attached to it. But they were, in fact, homeless people, away from their roots.

The word "depressed" is connected with the word "depression." But while the time of the Depression in our generation sometimes meant hunger and unemployment, in the now generation being depressed just means you have no fun.

The word "refugee" for the now generation is something connected with other countries. In our generation, we knew it was people being hunted and looking for a place to live.

We knew, because we shared their fears.

On the other hand, the word "affluence" was not used in our time, nor "doing your own thing."

You are right, I talk too much about the old generation.

But there is where I belong. I do not fit in with your vocabulary, which means your way of living. I am not "with it." Although saying the same words, we speak a different language.

I am still alive, but since I lost Bram, I feel and know that I belong to the old generation. Most of my generation has passed on, with their fears and lost hopes. And I feel left behind. I am a survivor.

But surviving is not the same as living. Surviving has its connection with the losses in the past. Living gives more hope for the future.

But I want the now generation to know about our trying, and our losses.

"We have the right to be understood!"

And because of that, I wrote this. Because the future generation, and the now generation, and the past generation, are from one chain, in which a survivor tries to be a link, to bring it together.

    For Bram and me
        Thank you.